D1394242

WINNING

HOW DONEGAL
CHANGED THE GAME
FOREVER

WINNING

HOW DONEGAL
CHANGED THE GAME
FOREVER

Rory Kavanagh
with
Liam Hayes

HEROBOOKS

HERO BOOKS

PUBLISHED BY HERO BOOKS
1 WOODVILLE GREEN
LUCAN
CO. DUBLIN
IRELAND
www.herobooks.ie
Hero Books is an imprint of Umbrella Publishing

First Published 2015

Copyright © Rory Kavanagh 2015
The moral rights of the author has been asserted
All rights reserved

Without limiting the rights under copyright reserved above, no part of this publication may be reproduced, stored in or introduced into a retrieval system, or transmitted in any form or by any means (electronic, mechanical, photocopying, recording or otherwise) without the prior written permission of the publisher of this book.

A CIP record for this book is available from the British Library

ISBN: 978-0-9526260-6-0

Printed in Ireland with Print Procedure Ltd
Cover design and typesetting: Jessica Maile
Cover photograph: Sportsfile
Photographs: Sportsfile and the Kavanagh family collection

To Kathryn and Zoe,
And in memory of Paula

ACKNOWLEDGEMENTS

Writing acknowledgements is a bit like working out how long is a piece of string. It's difficult to know exactly where to start and where to end, whilst of course trying not to forget anyone.

So many people have helped me along the way from there to here. I'm truly grateful for all the kindness and the support I have received.

I've had many great memories from my times involved in representing Ballyraine FC, Letterkenny and Donegal at Community Games. Thank you to all the coaches who were a big part of my life as a young player.

To all the coaches in St Eunan's GAA club who have worked with me over the years, thank you for helping me fulfil my potential. The time and effort these people put in means that, for me, they are the real unsung heroes.

Thanks to my teammates in St Eunan's, we continue to share a special bond.

To my close friends, thanks as always for your help and advice. And I would like to especially thank the principal and staff at my place of work, Scoil Cholmcille, who have been incredibly supportive.

When I announced my retirement from inter-county football in January, 2015, I received countless messages, whether cards or texts, wishing me luck. In fact, since making my debut with the Donegal seniors against Cork in Ballyshannon in 2001, people have always been loyal in their support of both the team and myself.

To the Donegal players and management, thanks for your honesty and effort. I have nothing but respect for you all.

Our medical teams were a vital part of our group. I, having spent a lot of time on the treatment table, valued the contribution they made to me personally. Through their expertise and valued advice, I was fit to perform in the most important games of my career.

I remember Liam Hayes and his brilliant Meath team of the late 1980s. Liam and I first made contact in the spring of 2015 and over the course of a great number of interviews and countless pots of tea, he has managed in an honest and insightful manner, to get my voice and thoughts onto paper.

I am fortunate to have the experience of working alongside someone like Liam who, as well as being a fantastic writer, has the understanding of the interior workings of a dressing room.

Thanks to his wife, Anne and the team at Hero Books for their key contributions to this book. And to my good friend and journalist, Alan Foley, thanks for the exhaustive hours as researcher and for helping me filling in the blanks. Annette Sweeney did a fantastic job with the photographs and thanks also to Elaine Gallagher, who provided sound contractual advice.

To all my extended family, a big thank you for all your support for me over the years. It always meant so much.

From New Line Road to Oaklands Park, where I grew up since the age of five, thanks to all the neighbours who have been really good to me.

To my sisters, Una, Tríona, Donna, Alma and my brother, Barry, needless to say you've always looked out for me – with me being the baby in the family! Thanks for all your love.

And to Mum and Dad, Agnes and Charlie, words aren't enough. Thank you for absolutely everything.

To Zoe, who is so full of life, you make us laugh and smile every day. And, finally, to Kathryn, thank you most of all, you have been at my side every step of the way.

Rory Kavanagh
September, 2015

'This is Donegal...
'These are our people!
'Out there...
'This is who we are!'

CONTENTS

PROLOGUE

I was listening to Jim McGuinness. It was August, 2010, and he was seated on a wide blue couch opposite me.

The couch was on the first floor, in an open area of the Clanree Hotel. He had come to Letterkenny to meet with me. He told me he was meeting with a number of players. In front of us was a large pot of tea and a plate of biscuits, but the biscuits were not touched.

Jimmy Tunes.

That's what we all called him.

And even though I was listening to what he had to say for himself for over an hour, and would continue to do so for another 30 minutes, this was still *Jimmy Tunes* who was sitting in front of me.

He had a black folder on the table. Inside the folder were lots of pieces of paper, things he wanted to show me. Mostly they were ideas of how he wanted Donegal to play.

Jim McGuinness was the new Donegal football manager. I was sceptical.

No doubt about that whatsoever. He had been appointed to the job a few weeks earlier, after his third time of asking to be Donegal football manager.

He wanted me to be bigger. He wanted to move me from a wing forward role to the middle of the field, and first of all, before then, he needed me to pack on an extra one and a half stone.

He wanted me in the middle of the field, and he wanted me defending. And he wanted me exploding out of defence with the ball, with men in front of me, either side of me.

That's not all he wanted.

He wanted me in the gym, straight away, even though the football year was still four months away. He told me I'd need to be in the gym five mornings each week. He was arranging for a gym in the town, for me and some of the other local boys. Michael Murphy would be in the same gym, and Karl Lacey, who had been moved to the Ulster Bank in Letterkenny and who was driving 40 minutes from Donegal Town each morning. We'd need to be in the gym before work each morning, seven o'clock in the morning.

He also wanted me to start eating more.

He wanted me to eat six times each day, minimum, and he told me what I had to eat. I was saying very little to him. I decided at the beginning of the meeting that this was a time to listen. To look him straight in the face, and mostly hear what he had to say. So, I hadn't very many questions for him.

He wanted me to snip the ties.

That's how he put it.

And that's what I remembered most of all after the one and a half hours. That request, which was really a totally serious demand.

'You've got to snip the ties...!'

He repeated himself on several occasions because, evidently, more than anything else, he wanted me to know that had to come first. I knew what he meant. He wanted my life to change. Football would have to come first. He wanted it to consume me more than anything else. There would be no more late nights

'Snip... the ties!'

I had said to myself that I would listen to everything he had to say for himself, and then I would make up my own mind.

But I wondered was he credible... was he... believable?

Jimmy Tunes?

Jim McGuinness?

The choice was mine, but after an hour and a half I was still not certain that I was prepared to give him all that he was asking from me.

Less than 12 months earlier, in the autumn of 2009, I'd been out on the field with him. Against him.

We were playing Naomh Conaill in the county final. McGuinness, as usual, was trying to influence proceedings, especially with the referee.

In the second half, he was going at it non-stop, and we were making sure that he kept it up. We would target him, no doubt. He was one of their leaders. We couldn't let him dictate the game.

'Referee... are you going to listen to this shite?

'... or are you going to ref the game yourself?'

McGuinness was gone. He had lost all discipline.

All composure, he had lost all intent of playing the game to win. Glenties had beaten us in the county final four years earlier, in 2005, when Jim McGuinness helped train the team under Hughie Molloy. Jim had a badly broken kneecap which kept him out of action for the second half of the season.

We got sucked into this deep defensive system he had them playing. They got their hands on the Dr Maguire Cup for the first time.

That county final in 2005 went to a replay. They had so many men behind the ball, and we could not break them down.

We also lost the county final in 2006 to Gaoth Dobhair in devastating fashion. Stephen Cassidy scored a goal in the dying minutes to beat us, the goal was almost like the one Seamus Darby scored against Kerry to sink Mick O'Dwyer's five in a row dream. To make matters worse, I had given the ball away when we were on the attack before that goal.

But we lifted Dr Maguire in 2007 when we beat Glenswilly by double scores, 0-12 to 1-3.

What a season 2007 was for St Eunan's. A massive achievement considering what had happened in 2005 and 2006. We had eight points to spare over Termon in the county final the following year, in 2008.

We were targetting an historic hat-trick of county titles against Naomh Conaill in the final in 2009.

As a team, St Eunan's had grown up early in 2007.

At the beginning of that year's championship, we had been sitting in the away dressing room in Glenties. We were after being destroyed. They had scored 5-6 in a first round, first leg championship game. A 17 year old Leo McLoone scored four goals.

After losing the county finals in 2005 and 2006 it seemed we had reached an almighty low. We were at a crossroads.

Where do we go from here?

What the hell happened out there?

We needed answers but there were none coming.

The silence was deafening.

I don't know why but I still felt that there had been some positives in the match. I actually thought we played quite well to begin with.

'We need to stick together now... more than ever,' I told the room.

The dressing room in O'Donnell Park in the minutes before taking the field against Glenties for the second leg of the first round tie was the most highly charged room I had ever stood in.

There was no chit chat, no jokes. Everyone was on edge. You could see it in everyone's eyes. This was it for us, for this team. We knew that. Everyone knew it. Our pride had been questioned. It was time.

That game was over before it even began. We won decisively, and made sure we brought the first round tie to a play off.

Us or Glenties? St Eunan's or Naomh Conaill?

Big winners or big losers?

'Right.... that's it....the next man to have a go at Rory Kavanagh is off.........'

I couldn't believe what I was hearing.

It was 10 minutes into the second half. Glenties were fighting for their lives, and they had me in their sights more than any other player it appeared.

The referee, Seamus McGonigle, finally had enough and issued his warning to the entire Glenties team.

He couldn't let it continue anymore. I was getting dog's abuse. But it took courage for Seamus to come out with his warning though. The tables had turned.

We had Glenties beaten. St Eunan's would march on in the championship... and keep marching for many years.

Jim McGuinness, in 2009, was joint manager of Glenties with Cathal Corey, and they swept into the final. It was our fifth county final in a row. We won 0-13 to 0-7 and we knew that we had seen the end of Jim McGuinness.

McGuinness and Brendan Devenney had been a pair.

They both liked their music and liked to DJ. McGuinness and Devenney were also big buddies.

Devenney was a livewire within the county squad. He was an outstanding footballer, and for a period of time he looked the most dangerous corner forward in the whole country.

I was quiet in the Donegal dressing room in those first couple of years. I was looking around me, taking it all in. Devenney was a clubmate, but was also a hero of mine since I was a little kid and wandered down to the field every weekend to see him play for St Eunan's. I remember him in the 1999 county final against Aodh Ruadh. Unplayable. Electrifying. He kicked 14 points to take St Eunan's to victory in what was a classic final. As youngsters, we talked about that game for months afterwards.

We had questions in our heads when Jim McGuinness got the Donegal job. The questions were all about the new manager.

Bloody hell.

That's what most of us were thinking. Has this man changed? Is this the man who is actually going to bring us to the Promised Land?

That was the biggest question most of the Donegal players were asking themselves? There were a large number of football careers that were about to disappear over the horizon. I knew I only had three or four years left myself. I had just turned 28 the same week McGuinness got the job, more or less, and I knew he was probably going to be my last chance.

I had been on the Donegal team for eight years. I'd spent four of those years waiting for my first championship start. For four years after that I had nailed down my place on the team and nailed it down good and proper, but I'd seen four Donegal managers come and go in those eight years.

He'd have to get his chance, the same as every other man before him but, frankly, after that first meeting in the Clanree Hotel I was still not feeling optimistic.

Clearly, McGuinness was able to read me at that first sit down, and in the months which followed on the training field and in meeting rooms, he could see that I was still living with some doubts about him.

We all had concerns, all of the senior players, and we talked about them every chance we got in the first few weeks and months.

I'd seen how Jim McGuinness worked as a coach and manager. I'd had first hand experience of that in the 2005 county final and replay, and all of us had watched him lead Donegal to the All-Ireland Under-21 final in 2010 where they got beaten by Dublin. He was strong minded, no doubt about that whatsoever. And he had a unique way of believing in how the game could be played.

That August morning, at our first meeting, in that open foyer on the hotel's first floor, he informed me that he had identified a priority group of footballers. There were seven or eight of us he wanted to meet with to begin with, but at the end of our one and a half hours the words sitting upright and demanding most attention was his request to snip the ties.

'Snip... THE TIES...!

'You want to... SNIP THE TIES... NOW!"

He said he saw me like him, in many ways, when he was in the middle of his Donegal career.

By then he'd told me he wanted me to grow into a midfielder. He'd told me all about the protype player he wanted on his team, and how he wanted his team to play. He wanted a big, strong, athletic team. He warned me it would be a shock to my system trying to pile on a stone and a half in weight, but that simply had to be done. The five mornings each week he wanted me to spend in the gym were already mapped out in detail, the weights, repetitions, sets.

My scepticism had hit its peak when he had opened his black folder, when he started drawing his sketches, showing me how we would play the game, how we would attack, how we would defend, first phase of defence, second phase of defence, third phase of defence, and how we would explode into attack. Thinking back on it now, it was impressive, and he was also massively true to his word, but at the time I needed to just walk away from him.

And think.

Make up my mind. I already knew what Michael Murphy thought about Jim McGuinness. Murph was McGuinness' Under-21 captain and he told any of us who asked him, that the man knew what he was doing.

Then there was my memory of Glenties in the 2005 county final.

Tackle, tackle, tackle, all high energy stuff from start to finish. That was Glenties in 2005 and they had beaten St Eunan's playing that brutally hard way, a way we had never quite seen in Donegal before then. We were being turned over in multiple tackles. And every time we were turned over, there was this huge roar from the crowd. That roar lifted them. I remember all of us being shocked at the level of energy Glenties brought into the game from the start to the finish.

Mickey Moran had brought me into the Donegal squad, but he'd never given me a championship start. He was a Derryman, but he was honest with us and he had nothing but the good of Donegal football at heart. And his sidekick John Morrison was a great coach.

I didn't get a championship start under Brian McEniff either. Brian was a legend in Donegal after winning our first senior All-Ireland title in 1992, a crowning glory, and all the more incredibly exquisite because a big bold Dublin team was defeated in the final. McEniff liked me, I thought, but he did not have absolute faith in me when any summer came. I was young, I was at St Patrick's College in Dublin training to be a primary school teacher and to be honest I wasn't fully committed to the cause.

Then there was Brian McIver in 2005. He was a serious character. I thought we were going places under McIver. He was ambitious, he'd won an All-Ireland club title with Ballinderry. He also believed in me, and believed in me enough to name me in his starting fifteen for his first championship game.

McIver took the job, resigned, and won the job a second time after having a change of heart.

Jim McGuinness wanted to be Donegal manager.

He had originally applied in 2007 but when Brian McIver changed his mind, that was that. In 2008, at his interview for the job in Ballybofey, McGuinness had been given assurances that he would have the facilties to show, on a PowerPoint presentation, his projections for Donegal football.

When he arrived, there was no plug socket in the room. He was told the interview would instead take a 'Question & Answer' format. I'm told he went ape shit.

He didn't get the job. But John Joe Doherty did.

As did Charlie Mulgrew! And Declan Bonner!

Wires had got crossed somewhere, somehow, and Doherty was offered the job, as was the Mulgrew-Bonner joint-ticket.

It was all too bizarre and ridiculous to be true, but it was true.

In the end, John Joe spoke from the heart to the clubs of the county. He got in.

John Joe was one of the heroes of '92 as well. He made me captain in 2009. But the cloud of controversy which was created at the time of his appointment never really blew away. John Joe Doherty was an emotional man.

He would have bled for the team, and he did.

Then we went from John Joe to Jim McGuinness.

In the autumn of 2010, I thought that we were swimming against the current. We were hammered by Armagh in the qualifiers, 2-14 to 0-11. The manner of the defeat bore similarities to the 1-27 to 2-10 loss against Cork in the All-Ireland quarter-final some 10 months beforehand.

It was probably the lowest of the low.

After Crossmaglen, we didn't know if we would play football for Donegal again. What was the point? We were listless. Colm McFadden was going to go. Kevin Cassidy was gone. The spirit in the team was torn asunder. Two brutal hammerings in a row, Cork in 2009, and then Armagh. What direction were we going?

No more than one month into Jim McGuinness' reign, I bumped into him in the middle of the night. It was more the early hours of the morning, to be honest. It must have been 1.30 in the morning, or later?

Our club was down in Dublin. We were playing in the Kilmacud Sevens football tournament the day before the All-Ireland final between Cork and Down in 2010. Our own county title was out of our hands by then. There was going to be no four in-a-row of Dr Maguire Cups! That Sunday night, or early Monday morning, I was with my clubmates, Mark McGowan and Conall Dunne. Conall and I had a few good years as Donegal footballers behind us, and he was as intrigued and bewildered by McGuinness' appointment as I was, although there had been no meeting between him and the new team boss.

Conall was getting what McGuinness had to say for himself second hand from me, as we were close friends. Though in the early hours of a Monday morning the immediate future of the Donegal football team was the last thing on our minds as we walked down the street to Coppers nightclub in the centre of the city. McGuinness had fixed a trial game for the next day, Monday night.

We bumped into Jim on our way into the nightclub.

He didn't seem so suprised to see the pair of us. We chatted away, grand.

'I'll see ye tomorrow night,' he said.

Myself and Conall met him again on the Monday evening as we walked towards the dressing rooms in Ballybofey. I was doing Jim's 'stations' by then in the gym, never missed one morning. Conall had asked me before we left Letterkenny if I thought he should play in the game?

He'd tweaked his hamstring a little bit during the Sevens in Kilmacud. I told him he'd be grand.

'He won't want you to do anything,' I said. And so there was only one bag with training gear in my car. I genuinely believed that Conall had nothing to worry about. He was one of the most dependable forwards in the county.

'Hey Jim... how's it going?'

'How are you doing, Jim?'

Each of us offered McGuinness a casual hello as we walked towards the dressing rooms. But McGuinness stopped us in our tracks.

'Where's your bag of gear?' he asked. He was looking at Conall.

'I didn't bring it, Jim,' replied Conall, '... twinged my hamstring down in Dublin, and... thought it might be better not to do more damage.'

Jim McGuinness did not look at him for very long before he started walking off in the opposite direction, but he did let Conall Dunne know exactly where he stood.

'This is the last trial game,' McGuinness declared.

'If you don't play tonight... you're not in my plans!'

Jim McGuinness was gone.

End of conversation. He never sat down with Conall Dunne, not once, and that was the only conversation they ever had between them. A month later, when the whole squad met up in Downings, for the first and perhaps the most significant meeting of Jim McGuinness' four years as Donegal team boss, Conall Dunne was nowhere to be seen. Jim McGuinness was the last Donegal manager he was ever going to meet.

That's f****** cut throat, I thought to myself.

That's no way to treat anybody.

McGuinness had the *Irish News* newspaper in one hand. He was standing by one of the large windows in the Rosapenna Hotel in Downings, and he was pointing out the window on a beautiful, crisp November morning.

He had already told us there was a football mad county out there dying to support the Donegal football team. He promised us that the people of Donegal were ready and prepared to follow us all over the country.

'If they have a team which shows real pride and ambition!' he declared.

An hour or so earlier he had opened the *Irish News* and, for maximum effect, he had visibly chewed on the number 19 in front of us all. The newspaper had ranked us 19th in the country. McGuinness wanted to know why?

He wasn't blaming the journalists in the newspaper. He wanted us to tell him why they would decide that Donegal were only fit to be named the 19th best team in the country?

'Tell me why?' he asked.

He had us broken into groups of five and six, and told us to come back to him with what we knew. And we did that. We told him why somebody might decide that we were no better than 19th. He didn't argue with us. He accepted what we told him.

Then he was at the window.

He was pointing out at the sea, and the wildness of the waves. And he pointed at the hills and the mountains, and the wee homes dotted all over the headlands of Sheephaven Bay. The newspaper was in one hand dropped down by his waist and the other hand had a finger pointing far outside.

'This is Donegal,' he told us.

'These are our people!' he declared, '... out there... this is who we are!'

It was more than interesting to see him at work.

McGuinness was inspirational for those few minutes and on my way home that evening, I thought, *maybe.*

Maybe this man has something.

Jim McGuinness had awoken our senses at that first group meeting, and by the end of it most of us were firmly of a mind to run up all of the hills he was pointing out at, and knock on the doors of every home in sight and tell the Donegal folk in there that we were going to be a team that was going to make them so proud as a people.

More than anything else, he did not want us to think that he was someone full to the brim with emotion, dreaming wildly of what could be?

He told us everything that was in his head.

We'd be running over the dunes in Dunfanaghy in November and December, he promised, though he did not tell us that he would have boys on the tops of the peaks of the dunes, like Maxi Curran who was part of our backroom team, with a video recorder.

Nobody wanted to have a video recorder in their face when they thought they were about to throw up on any dune, any second, but in July 2011, hours before taking the field against Derry in the Ulster final, those recordings topped us up with certainty. Maxi Curran had put together a short motivational video containing some of our best moments on the pitch together with some of our worst on the dunes! It filled us with belief.

The dune running was tough, but a welcome change from the monotony of doing laps of a field. You needed your wits about you too. Running over uneven ground meant that the placing of every single stride was important to maintain a smooth flow to your running. Coming back down the dune could be treacherous especially if the man in front was going at a slower pace.

One sight I remember vividly at the end of one gruelling dune session was that of Barry Dunnion being physically carried back to the changing rooms by two members of the back room team. His legs had gone on him and he had trouble standing up. It was slightly unnerving to watch as one of the fittest lads I knew was being carried off the dunes.

We left every last drop we had out there on those dunes and a good part of our breakfast too! The stillness of the crisp winter air would be frequently pierced with the sound of wretching from doubled over bodies at the end of each lung busting run. And then would come the call from a member of the backroom team, it was time to go again.

Christ! I thought. *I have nothing left.*

It was a test for the body but more for the mind. An extra run would be added if we didn't meet the required time on the completion of each run. No cutting corners, no excuses. Survival of the fittest.

I remember after one of these sessions driving home to Letterkenny and sitting in my car outside my house for what felt like an hour. I couldn't muster up the energy to get out. So I just closed my eyes and sat there, my limbs aching and my mind willing my body to be still, to rest.

The one thing we could not make head nor tails of, however, was how Jim McGuinness and Rory Gallagher suddenly got together. Myself and Big Neil could not work it out. Michael Murphy was just as clueless. Colm McFadden, Jim's own brother in law, was no help.

How did the two of them hook up?

Gallagher was living and working in Killybegs and had trained the local GAA club at Fintra a couple of times. Martin McHugh had heard positive stories of his approach and recommended him to McGuinness.

I think it was just a quick phone call.

Peter McGinley from Killybegs had worked with McGuinness on the Under-21s but he had to suddenly pull out of the backroom team because of work commitments. From what I'm told, they met in Letterkenny one night over that cold Christmas in 2010. They arranged to meet for an hour and ended up chatting football half the night.

Rory Gallagher was just as quickly McGuinness' No.2.

In the days leading into the Ulster semi final against Tyrone in 2012, when we were reigning Ulster champions, and badly needed to stamp our authority down upon Mickey Harte and his team a second time, and in double quick order, I was carrying a left leg. My left ankle, eternally troubling me, had blown up again. I had missed the quarter final match with Derry in Ballybofey when the team produced a great performance. I remember watching on and thinking this is going to be a battle now to regain my place. Not one player had a bad game. And the midfield pairing of Ryan Bradley and Neil Gallagher had done especially well.

If a man was missing from the training field in the second last week before a championship game then there was a high chance he would be a liability in Jim's book.

But not this time.

Rory Gallagher rang me a few days before the game against Tyrone. He asked me how I was?

'I'm good to go, Rory... I'm ready to play!'

He told me that McGuinness did not want to start me, as he had doubts.

'Don't worry... you'll be starting!' he promised.

When the team was named I was amongst the long list of substitutes trailing after the first 15. I was No. 19.

No. 19 started against Tyrone. I scored two points.

They were, at times, like two prized scholars bouncing ideas off one another. They'd start... Jim going on and on about defensive shape, and Rory jumping in with counter attacking options, over and back, Jim, Rory, Jim, Rory... they were unstoppable.

They could not stop talking at times like that. Huddles on the field could become a nightmare for us. They'd talk for far too long. We might be a half an hour or 45 minutes into our session, and they'd start.

We'd be all grouped tightly around them, listening, and then getting cold, and fed up, and wishing they'd just shut up.

But they were always brilliant.

I loved watching Ryan Bradley during the huddles. He would be rolling his eyes to the Heavens and giving out no end after it had stopped.

'F*** sake.'

'Are you stiff?' he would ask. 'Jesus they never shut up... do they?'

And off he would run shaking his head and trying to loosen himself up again.

Rory and Jim clearly started to grow apart through 2013 when we had an All-Ireland title on our hands that needed defending, and the stakes were raised for all of us, brought to a height none of us had ever imagined would be our place in the football world. It was a new place for Jim and Rory in their relationship as well.

There were signs, maybe, that tension was there. Like the banquet night in the Mount Errigal Hotel in December, 2012. We were all to receive our Ulster and All-Ireland medals. When Jim and Rory went to receive their medals, however, there was one for Jim, but none for Rory.

Rory wasn't a happy camper. If there was no medal for Rory why wasn't he told before going up on the stage? I felt bad for him, all the boys did.

By the end of the year, our Ulster title was taken from us by Monaghan in the provincial final, and Mayo had taken a fierce retribution in scoring 4-17 in the All-Ireland quarter final and did all they could to try to amend the massive loss they suffered at our hands in 2012.

By the end of 2013, Jim and Rory also ended up physically apart.

I'm told that Jim had given Rory and Maxi a firm handshake at a club championship game in Letterkenny and told them they were going their separate ways.

Jim McGuinness did not explain why to the people of Donegal, and he did not sit down with his players either. We were all left in the dark together, picking up the pieces, talking to one another, wondering exactly what Jim was thinking? Damien Diver, John Duffy and Paul McGonigle formed his new think tank.

None of that surprised me really. Jim McGuinness, I knew in my heart, always, would do the job in an absolutely professional, but cut throat manner.

I knew when it came to the end, that's how it would be. Of course he talked about us all meeting up later in life, 10 years down the road or whatever, and being able to have a pint, being able to look one another in the eye, and maybe not having to say very much.

Maybe saying nothing at all.

I was sitting at home with Kathryn on a Friday night in early October, 2014, when I was informed that Jim McGuinness had resigned as Donegal football team manager.

Almost two weeks had passed since the All-Ireland final defeat by Kerry, but the gut-wrenching disappointment had still not entirely left my body. I turned to Kathryn, who was holding our little daughter, Zoe when the text message came through from him.

'He's gone...!'

Kathryn was a little bit surprised. I was less so. Big Neil and I were chatting most days about it. I warned Big Neil that McGuinness was going! I told him that he was not coming back for one more year.

Big Neil wasn't so sure. He thought it would be hard, perhaps impossible, for the man to walk away after losing an All-Ireland final. Big Neil did not think Jim would want to live with that pain, and would surely choose to give one more year in order to kill off the doubts and 'what ifs' and all of the other nonsense which invades a man's head after a supreme loss in a game of football.

'Nah... I'm telling you... he'll not come back!'

I felt that instinctively.

'Well Men,'... his text began.

It took a while for the message to sink in.

So I read it again. We had been on an unbelievable journey for four years. Reading the text message just brought home the reality that this was indeed the end.

Thoughts of how I would reply rumbled through my mind half the night. But what do you say to someone like that? It was difficult to sum up just what I was feeling. The next morning, I put a text message together thanking Jim for what he had done for me and I wished him the very best for the future.

We knew him as a manager, and as a protector. He would defend us as individuals and as a team, at the drop of a hat. Sometimes he would be fairly irate when others disrespected us.

In his four years with us, we came to know McGuinness so well. But I can not say I knew the man personally, or had any insight to the depths of his mind.

But we got to see his private side.

Each time we claimed the Ulster title, in 2011, '12 and '14, and when we brought Sam Maguire home in 2012 also, the team bus would stop on the road outside of Donegal, near Lisnaskea in Fermanagh, where Jim McGuinness had lost his brother, Mark. The bus would stop and Jim would get out with the cup and place it in front of the cross positioned on the side of the road.

Mark McGuinness, a couple of years older than Jim, had been driving his brother to the airport a few weeks after Donegal had lost to Derry in the 1998 Ulster final to an agonising late goal from Joe Brolly. 1-7 to 0-8.

Jim decided to play ball in America for the rest of the summer. The car accident took Mark's life a few weeks after the game. The car had gone into a spin. He was the second brother Jim had lost. Another brother, Charles had died from a heart condition a decade earlier.

Jim would place the cup in front of the cross dedicated to Mark and stand there for a few minutes. In prayer, I guess. We all watched from the windows of the bus. We were all quiet for those few minutes. None of the players, however, joined Jim at the side of the road.

It was his private moment.

During the four years we spent together, we all had our faith. Belief in one another, and a need to talk to loved ones no longer with us.

For me, it was my sister, Paula.

Wee Paula was born three years before me, but was only with our family for a couple of months. She died a cot death, as they described it for so many years. I visited Paula's grave before so many games, and in quiet moments I would chat with her, and ask her to help me.

I'd let her know how we were doing, what we were doing as a family, how I had a game of football which I had to win.

But I never shared my conversations with Paula with anybody else on the team. It was absolutely none of their business. We were teammates and the tightest of friends, but we all had our private lives as well.

Jim McGuinness, I imagine, needed that private place more than anybody.

I'd grown to like him more. Every year that increased. Over the four years I also understood Jim McGuinness' ways as a football manager.

Initially, that annoyance, that tetchiness which resided within me due to the rivalry between St Eunan's and Glenties, obscured things in the opening months. By the summer of 2011, however, he had me fully intrigued. After that, Jim McGuinness had me, like he had everyone else in the dressing room, mystified at times, but absolutely willing to run my entire life to his grand plans.

He changed my life.

He thanked us in his final text message. It is a pity that most of us have never had a chance to formally thank him back. Or tell him, face to face, that he is a man and a leader who will always remain in our lives.

I look forward to having that word with him.

Sometime. Who knows?

Or, perhaps, there are words which we will never need to utter. Words can appear like a full stop. And some relationships are not in need of a full stop.

2011

CHAPTER

'That's what f****** living is!'

Jim McGuinness had us all huddled around him in the middle of the field in Croke Park. Our All-Ireland quarter final against Kildare was not long over. Ten minutes, I'd guess. We had won by a single point. The floodlights still had the amazing stadium fully illuminated, though most of the supporters were gone. Kildare had left the field too.

McGuinness was pumped nevertheless.

We were all running on close to empty as we stood around him. Donegal and Kildare footballers had been fighting off cramp, or else collapsing to the ground, through the second half of extra time. One of the Kildare boys had fallen right beside me, as though someone from the stands had shot him from a couple of hundred yards away.

'That was epic...

'That was f****** awesome... BOYS!'

There was an electricity coursing through McGuinness. It was rampaging through us as well, seeking to revive us. He told us we did not realise the significance of the game we had just won.

'That was pure..!' he exclaimed.

The game itself, although it had just finished, was a crazy mixture of scores and tackles, a thrilling roller-coaster ride that seemed like it might never end. My late tackle resulted in a free and Kildare getting the equalising score to send the game to extra time.

Christy Toye's goal was his first touch in 25 months. Injury after injury. He'd been through hell. The character of the man to come back!

Kildare's last burst to try to win.

Kevin Cassidy's point which finally did it. That roaring last point of the game from Cass was like a point ordered up by the Gods.

The rain was coming down harder as we remained out on the field with McGuinness, and the wetness and the powerful lights made the men standing around me look like Superheroes. We had fought for our lives, and something more than that. We had fought and won, and put an end to all of the near misses and colossal failures that had been part of our lives up to that evening in Croke Park. For once, for the very first time, we had engaged in an epic contest and come out the other side as winners.

We had crossed the line and arrived somewhere new to us. Everyone was bolloxed. Everyone had cramped badly in extra time. On one occasion, I had attempted to take off and both of my calves seized up on me.

Each time I cramped, I stopped for a little while. Stood there and tried to stretch just a little. I'd try to run again, slowly.

I'd trot and then be able to take off.

But I was unable to take off from a standing start during the final 10 minutes of the game. I had nothing left.

I was closer to empty than I had ever been in my life.

'That's what f****** living is!'

It was Tyrone, not Armagh who sat centre stage in Jim McGuinness' mind from the very beginning.

It was, of course, Armagh more than any other team who had entirely sickened Donegal over the eight mostly dispiriting years I had spent in the county dressing room. My first championship season was 2002. Armagh beat us that year, as they did in 2003, 2004, 2005 and 2006. Then, of course, there was Crossmaglen in 2010.

Mickey Harte was Jim McGuinness' No. 1 target.

In January, in Jim McGuinness' first month as Donegal manager, we lost to Tyrone in the McKenna Cup. We also lost to Fermanagh by the end of the month in Ballybofey and our hopes of winning three McKenna Cups in a row were gone. McGuinness didn't give a damn.

'Do any of ye...' he asked the dressing room, '... really think you are going to be counting up McKenna Cups?

'... or... do you think at the end of your careers...

'anybody... anybody at all is going to ask you how many McKenna Cups you managed to win?'

We agreed. It would be a nonsense question.

We'd played Tyrone in Edendork.

The pitch was frozen over that day, and it was hard to breathe it was so perishingly cold by the time the ball was thrown up into the air. The game was supposed to have been in Omagh, but was switched at the last minute because the ground in Omagh was even harder than the ground in bloody Edendork. We changed in a portacabin. But who was going to feel sorry for us?

Mickey Harte had buried his daughter, Michaela only a few weeks earlier after the poor girl was murdered on her honeymoon in Mauritius. He led Tyrone out onto the field. And there were a few thousand Tyrone supporters there to greet him more than his team.

They won 1-13 to 0-13. A week later we lost by five points to Fermanagh. But McGuinness wasn't unhappy. He hadn't showed his hand to Harte in Edendork. We were told to play the game we always played. No massed defence, nothing new, nothing different from half forwards and midfielders. Then, in the middle of February, we travelled to Healy Park and defeated Tyrone by seven points in the league.

The only time I had seen Mickey Harte up close was back in 2007 when he came to talk to St Eunan's in the build up to the county final. We had lost three county finals since 2001. We were being labelled as 'chokers' and we were playing our neighbours and rivals, Glenswilly.

The management recognised that handling the pressure of the big day was an issue for us and they were determined to do everything they could.

Mickey was a class act.

He talked to us for over an hour, going into detail on how he managed the Tyrone team in the build up to the 2003 All-Ireland final against Kerry. He emphasized the need to distance ourselves from all distractions.

Families, friends, trips into town, the lot! It was the first time we had met Glenswilly in a county final and the buzz around the town was enormous. Everyone was talking about the game.

'Let the club members enjoy the build up…!'

That's what Mickey told us.

'But you… YOU have a match to win!'

First and foremost, he told us to stay in each other's company, and to avoid energy sappers; boys who just want to talk football non stop!

As for the on-field stuff, he coined a term I would never forget, and which visited my head in big bold letters every time I ever played against Tyrone after that.

'Psycho for the ball'.

Harte said that he coached his players to become 'psychos for the ball' and he used Ryan McMenamin as an example in describing the determination with which his players hunted down man and ball.

Afterwards Mickey sat patiently answering questions from all of our players and I have no doubt that meeting played a big role in us winning that county final. He didn't ask for a penny for the trip down, and he made a big impression on the whole group.

To be fair to the St Eunan's team management and our manager, Brendan Kilcoyne they were pulling out all the stops to get us mentally prepared.

We beat Glenswilly in 2007, 0-12 to 1-3.

We would go on to win three county titles in a row but, more importantly, we haven't lost a final since 2006.

Victory over Tyrone had emboldened us as a group.

We played Kildare close to the end of the month, in my home pitch in Letterkenny, and in front of my family and all of my friends, and a goodly number of Donegal supporters, the McGuinness way of looking to become a winning football team almost worked to perfection. Our message that day was simple.

Stop them at source.

Make contact and do not let them get running at us.

We scored eight points. It was 0-8 to 0-4 after Michael Murphy shot over the point of the game in the 68th minute, and we should have switched the game off at that point. Closed it down, and sent everyone home. We knew how hard it had been to get that lead that afternoon against Kildare. It had taken us 17 minutes to get our first score, and that was a free kick from Colm McFadden.

But in the final minute of the game, Kildare had kicked a late point. And there was only a goal in it. The game went into injury time.

A free from Johnny Doyle, somehow, worked its way into the hands of their full back Mick Foley who was looking to be a hero and save the game.

Foley fired it into the corner of the net.

Kildare undid our whole day's work in a couple of minutes and grabbed a draw. By April, we had a Division Two final against Laois to look forward to, but it was in the harsh draw with Kildare that Jim McGuinness was certain we had gained something of absolutely immense value.

After that game in Letterkenny he came up with a plan to ensure that we would never foolishly throw away a win ever again. Or risk anybody stealing a win from us.

McGuinness had a list of 20 key performance indicators which, he insisted, told him the whole story of every game.

At least, he believed, it told him everything about us.

Each of the 20 indicators had to receive a score out of five, one being poor, five being excellent. The first five indicators centred on our defensive performance. The next three or four usually told the story of the battle to win the ball in the middle of the field and the success of our kick outs, and after that it was about how we went about winning the game at the other end of the field. But the last indicator was always rock solid gold in McGuinness' eyes.

No.20 asked us to judge our... 'Belief in The System'.

Our belief as footballers in what our manager was asking us to do in every aspect of our game. Jim would break us all up into groups of four or five, with six or seven players in each group, and he would send us off to mark off the 20 indicators and then report back to him.

We always tackled the job at hand with one hundred per cent seriousness, as vitally important as the game itself the previous Sunday.

We'd get into deep discussions.

'Did we keep our defensive shape?

'You two are saying we did... I'm not too sure!

'So we sprinted back to exactly where we needed to be on every breakdown... is that agreed?

'Boys... out of FIVE...?

'What are we giving ourselves?

'Are we saying we sprinted back every time?

'How well did we transition out of defence?

'Were there men getting ahead of the ball?

'Are we saying five... saying four... are we saying FOUR?

'There were four or five examples in the first half... in the second?

'Two... three... wasn't the same, was it?

'What are we putting down... two?

'Are we saying... TWO?

'I'm putting down two... agreed?

'AGREED?'

And that's the way each group would run through each of the 20 indicators. Jim and Rory Gallagher would be at the top table, and they were also marking down numbers at the same time. Then it was time for each group to appoint a voice to call out the results.

If there were big discrepancies between different groups, then McGuinness wanted answers. He'd want to know why we wrote down a big number? He liked to back us up, and make us question ourselves in front of the whole, wider grouping.

It was an excellent way of understanding fully how the team had performed, and it helped me to know for sure what Jim McGuinness was asking from me in my busy role. It was black and white, no greyness. And it was a public discussion, no one on one stuff enacted quietly to the side. Each and every one of us would end up in the dock at some stage in these discussions. The numbers one and two would be written down often enough, we'd no trouble doing that, and that displayed the honesty within the team.

God help, however, the man chosen as leader of a group who marked their belief in the system a full, bold figure five. In those early months it took balls for anyone to do that. McGuinness would stand up occasionally when he saw a five. And then he'd start.

'How did you mark that a five?

'Tell me... you're telling me that your belief in our system of play is a five, is that what you're telling me Rory Kavanagh?

'If you f****** believed in the system you would have sprinted back and you would have stopped that score...

'... you would have been where you were supposed to be!

'You would have been where you are supposed to be in our defence... if you actually believe in our system.

'Rory Kavanagh... if you believed in the system, you would have broken the ball down... instead of trying to catch it.

'F****** go and break the f****** thing...

'Why did you try to catch the ball... if you believe in what we are trying to do here? Why didn't you smash the ball back into their defence?

'If you believed in the system... Rory... if you believed in the system you'd have smashed it 20 yards back... and you're saying to me...

'You're seriously telling me... that you believe in the system?'

'You do not believe in the system...

'So... don't be giving yourself high marks for believing in the system when I know... when I can see on this DVD we've looked at... that you do not believe in the system!'

More than anything else during that first league campaign, McGuinness had learned that his team needed to know the difference between defending, and defending with our lives on the line. He had learned it in Letterkenny when Mick Foley scored Kildare's last gasp goal.

We needed to know the difference.

He felt, that first year, but only during that first year, that he needed to spell it out for us. Big posters were printed out which showed exactly how our system worked, and how that system could change, and could become even more increasingly defence-driven during games.

We had a 56.

That meant that we were getting mostly everyone behind the ball, every single time our opponents won back possession. We would have two men in the opposing half of the field.

We had a 56 + 1.

That was every single man back, apart from one solitary figure in the other half. And then, precisely because of the Mick Foley goal, McGuinness introduced a new number. It was a 6.

Once 6 was roared from the sideline, or if Rory Gallagher raced onto the field as our runner and shouted... '6... 6... 6....!' that meant that ever single man was to get behind the ball immediately. And stay there.

The number 6 was... lockdown.

The number 6 meant stop them from scoring a goal and take our win. Number 6 meant they owned the field, and they owned the ball pretty much, but number 6 meant they were not going to get any shots off within 21 yards of our goals. Number 6 meant we were holding onto our win.

Number 6 meant we were risking nothing.

We won the Division Two league final, sweetly defeating Laois by a single point in Croke Park close to the end of April, and gaining revenge for the tumbling we'd taken from them in Portlaoise two weeks earlier. Jim McGuinness ensured we had enough beer on the bus for the journey home.

The journey on the way home was great craic. We had a team that could sing a song or two. Some of us took our turns to sing at the top of the bus. Christy Toye would do an Oasis number, mine would be *American Pie*.

Dermot 'Brick' Molloy and Leo McLoone were comedy gold. They could take off anyone. Leo would do Shaun Doherty of Highland Radio and Brick would be a concerned listener. They were brilliant and kept the whole bus entertained on the way home

Jim had a few beers himself. He was in flying form, as we all were. McGuinness had this great booming laugh that would reverberate around the whole bus. It was a laugh that drowned out all the conversations. The same laugh would become a familiar sound on many trips over the years. He needed his down time too and he understood more than most what we needed.

After significant wins he had no trouble allowing us to enjoy each other's company, and squeeze some extra craic out of the victory. He'd be relaxed himself, and become a different man for a few hours.

Monday evening was for recovery from the game, not from a night's heavy drinking. It wasn't like the old days when, after every second interesting win, two or three boys would scoot off for 48 hours.

From early in 2011, we'd be in the swimming pool or in hydrotherapy, or getting a rub down on a Monday evening. A jacuzzi would be waiting for us after the chilling iced water. We'd have a gentle swim. And get ready for Tuesday evening. But, as we journeyed home from Dublin after the league win, we were all more than satisfied with ourselves. The few beers helped raise the roof of the bus that bit higher.

A voice from the front of the bus, however, suddenly demanded quietness. It sounded like Jim.

Michael Hegarty had the mic in his hand.

'Jim here... !' he shouted.

Hegarty could have been Jim McGuinness. When I heard him, before looking up at him, I thought it was Jim McGuinness.

'Hold on there a second boys... BOYS... just halt your drinking there a wee second...

'JIM HERE...!' he repeated himself. 'I'm calling a 56... do you hear me?

'Actually... I'm thinking... I'm calling a 56 + 1...

'No... WAIT...

'... WAIT... BOYS WAIT...

'It a... F****** LOCKDOWN... I'M CALLING

'... I'M CALLING ...

'...A

'... 6!'

The first time I wore a Donegal jersey I was 17 years old, and that evening I came home with a pair of county shorts and socks, no jersey. We had lost to Monaghan in the first round of the Ulster minor championship.

I felt a hero all the same.

I hadn't played very well, but I understood that I had taken my place in a long, long line of young and older men who had worn the greatest green and gold jersey in the world. There might have been thousands and thousands of men, but I was one of them.

Anthony Molloy, the man who had captained the county to its only All-Ireland win in 1992, was our team manager. James McHugh, another man who had won the greatest prize in the game, was his assistant.

Playing for Donegal was serious stuff. It was the greatest honour any young man could ever win for himself. Though when I pulled that championship jersey over my head in Ballybofey I felt smothered by the size of the same honour. It was like a dream. My brain was flooded with high hopes. And the game began and ended at one hundred miles per hour.

I've no idea how I played, to be honest. Everything went out the window once the ball was thrown up. I was in the middle of the field. But the number on my back did not matter. It was the jersey that mattered. I had inherited something money could not buy.

I had crossed a threshhold as a young man.

It was a scorcher of a day. My heart was forcing its way out of my chest before I even left the dressing room. In the game that followed Monaghan pulled away from us in the second half. Paul Finlay kicked two or three frees that won the game for them.

When I played Under-21 for Donegal, Brian McEniff's son, Seanie was in charge, and then Mickey Moran took over the year after him. We beat Derry that second year, lost to Cavan. And when Mickey Moran was named Donegal senior manager he named me on his first squad. There was so much talent on those minor and Under-21 teams. Karl Lacey, Kevin Rafferty, Kevin Cassidy, Christy Toye, Colm McFadden, Eamon and Neil McGee, boys who were outstanding footballers in my mind. But we won nothing. At minor and Under-21 we did not know how to win games that really mattered.

We did not work hard enough in training. We did not know how hard we should work, or we chose not to, it didn't matter much, because we were too damned nice as footballers.

We accepted things that happened on the field. When things went against us we did not fight back. There was no hard edge.

We were Donegal people.

The same people Jim McGuinness identified at his first team meeting in Downings, when he pointed out the large window.

We were all softly spoken. As footballers, there was nothing nasty about us. We'd no idea how to be street-smart on a football field. As young men we did not know what we needed to do to win every game. When it really mattered, we fell on our faces. We crumbled. We went into ourselves, and never stood up. The Tyrones and the Armaghs and any team worth its salt knew that Donegal would not stand up. Not when everything was on the line.

They knew we would submit.

We did not think like winners.

Make no mistake about it, beating Laois in a final was a big game for us all. Playing in Croke Park was a big deal to us back then and would remain so. A National title was on the line.

We had to earn our place in Croke Park.

But, above all, we had to show that we were a team going in the right direction under Jim McGuinness and winning the title sent out that message.

It was a game we didn't want to lose.

With 10 minutes left they had narrowed the gap to just one point. We responded well with points from Colm, Cass and myself. That response was a big moment in the year for us, just like the fightback against Sligo was in our very first league game and we had managed to draw with them. We had shown true resolve when the pressure was on.

The team was building character.

CHAPTER 2

To make the system work, the team relied so heavily on Nos. 8 and 9, and 10 and 12. Usually the six backs had licence to race forward at any time, and it was the responsibility of the midfielders and the wing forwards to maintain our defensive shape. Whoever was centre-forward also had a primary role as the system was further strengthened.

As the system further developed it didn't matter who was sitting so long as we had five back at all times. That job usually fell to Neil McGee and it wouldn't be uncommon to see him grab one or two players by the scruff of the neck in training and tell them to sit if he felt no one was listening to him!

And Murph, soon enough, would also become an instrumental part as the system was refined, further refined in 2012, and refined again in 2014. The greatest footballer in the game, and also the greatest scoring forward in the game. But Murph also fell back into defence.

My role was to man mark someone with a big name, or a crucial role on the opposing team. Work my way up the field and turn the tables on whoever I was marking by grabbing at least one or two points in every game. And, every time the ball was lost, or any time we turned it over, I had to get back and take up my position in our defence.

By the start of the 2011 championship the McGuinness system was still a work in progress. It was raw as hell.

My mother loved her candles.

She also loved dousing me in holy water before every game. My gear bag would also get a fair wetting. In our home a Blessed Candle was always lit if anyone was sick, or if it was exam time, or if one of us was taking a driving test. Blessed candles were aimed high and low by my mother to get the right results.

The wee candle always sat on the windowsill in the kitchen. With me, too, a lot of my mother's worries were rooted in the fact that I was the youngest in the family, and I had arrived into her arms three years after my sister, Paula died after eight weeks in a cot death. Paula died in May of 1979. I was born in 1982 and my mother, Agnes Bonner, a Burt woman from the base of the Inishowen peninsula, hurling country God help them, was simply over-protective of me.

She was a worrier.

So many Blessed Candles were lit, and so many prayers were said during my childhood, and these continued into my footballing years. She would be sitting at the kitchen table when I came into the house on a Friday evening and she'd know I would be away to Dublin for a game on the Saturday morning.

'God save us and bless us...... make sure and win.'

'But...,' she'd then say, just to get it straight with the Man above, '... it doesn't matter, not as long as you come back safe!'

There were seven of us in the family. Una, Tríona, Donna, Alma, Barry, Paula... and me. My Dad, Charlie was a Convoy man, and he was a strong, calming influence in our home. He worked in the VEC and then did some taxi work in his post-retirement years. My mother worked in Letterkenny hospital for 25 years.

So, when Brian McEniff began to march Donegal to the All-Ireland title in 1992, my mother was as much my protector, as ever. I remember being at some games as a small child. I know I was sandwiched between my father and one of his mates more than once. I remember the supporters' bus. The tea and home made sandwiches. I also have vivid memories of being hooshed over a wall in Breffni Park before one championship game.

But I did not get to the Ulster final in '92, and neither was I included in the ticket handout before the All-Ireland final against Dublin. The rest of the family all got tickets, including Barry and all of my sisters. I was designated to stay at home and 'mind' my mother.

We watched the game on our TV. Afterwards, I ran out onto the street and there were horns going and soon enough I was away up the town following the noise. I remember sitting on the bonnet of one car and I was draped in a flag and my mother, still caring for me on this day of all days, was not far behind.

The team arrived into Letterkenny, led by McEniff and Anthony Molloy, on the Tuesday night. There were thousands of people still drinking and making more noise than I imagined possible at 10 years of age. I sat on my father's shoulders all evening long, and he never complained once.

Donegal had not won an Ulster championship match in four years. So, Sunday, May 15, was a day that nobody was truly welcoming. It was a wet, miserable morning in Ballybofey. There was the fear of losing to Antrim in the preliminary round of the championship. And, then, for me, there was the additional fear that I simply would not be able to do, for 70 minutes, exactly what Jim McGuinness was asking from me. Four awful years.

We were Division One league champions back in 2007 when we snatched a very late goal to get by Armagh. In the Ulster semi final we got chucked out on our ear by Tyrone.

We had lost to Derry in 2008, Antrim in '09 when I was captain, and Down in 2010. Now we had Antrim on our hands. Again. And, at home, which meant that we were going to have to get McGuinness' high octane gameplan one hundred per cent right in front of all of our own people.

Could I do everything Jim McGuinness was demanding? Could all of the boys carry it out? There were questions jumping up and down in more heads than just mine.

I had put on the weight that I was told to put on, and I had been eating like there was no tomorrow. I was at the gym at seven in the morning, every morning before work. I was taking a shake, gobbling down my cereal and heading off to the gym. I was taking another shake after the session. At 10.40 or 11.0 am, at the first break in school I would eat a chicken sandwich. I'd eat a second chicken sandwich at lunchtime. My dinner was at 4.0, immediately when I got home from work. And I'd be eating a big enough supper at 8.0 if I was not training, or else after our evening session.

That's the way my life had been since I had met McGuinness in the Clanree Hotel in August. It was hard to be eating all of the time. The only things that I enjoyed were the power smoothies, banana, kiwi, pineapple, two scoops of protein whey, bit of orange juice. Shake it all up and I was on my way. Not half as time consuming as watching chicken boil.

I was eating around the clock, training harder than I had ever trained in my life, and I never felt so unfit.

To do everything Jim McGuinness wanted done, in the middle, at the back, up front, but always getting back without fail, never letting him or any of the boys on the pitch down, to do all of that for 70 minutes?

I was half terrified that I would not be able to get through it. Mentally, in the days and then the hours before running out onto the field in Ballybofey to play Antrim, I felt overwhelmed. I did not feel myself. The first stone had been piled on really sharpish. Jim and Rory wanted me up on the scales every second day in the gym. I had been 12 stones and 10 pounds when we had our chat in the Clanree Hotel. The morning of the first round of the championship, I was tipping 14 stones.

All of that damned chicken!

It was expensive, for starters. McGuinness had all of the supplements handed out to us, but the chicken was part of our own weekly shopping bill. I was buying chicken and eggs to beat the band. And, every night, I had to make sure all of my food for the next day was prepared, my breakfast smoothies, my snack for the first break at school, my lunch, my dinner after school. There had to be more to life than boiling chicken fillets round the clock.

By the time we met Dublin, in the All-Ireland semi final in 2014, in a game that had the whole country enthralled, against opponents who were deemed simply unbeatable, we did not have a fear in the world.

The first evening we met up, after that semi final pairing was decided, Jim McGuinness told us that he knew how to beat Dublin.

'I have been tracking these boys... all year!' he informed us, before bringing us out onto the training field. 'And... I know how to beat them!'

'All this talk about Dublin... it's all bullshit.

'... BULLSHIT...!'

That afternoon in late summer, 2014, in the All-Ireland semi final, we played 3, 2, 3, 4 in front of Paul Durcan. The full backs had their man marking jobs. Ryan McHugh and always one other half forward was sweeping in front of the full back line. There were three half backs in front of them, and then there were four of us, including me, sweeping over and back just inside our 45 metres line.

It was a compact, water-tight defence, but every single man in that defence was also itching to race into the other half of the field and tear apart what was left of the Dublin defence. We all knew exactly how we were going to defend against them and destroy Dublin in 2014.

When we had played Dublin in 2011, in the All-Ireland semi final, we only knew half as much about ourselves and our own ability as a team. That is the honest truth. In that ugly semi final in 2011, which we lost by two late points, Jim McGuinness' system was really only half built.

It was so different in 2014.

McGuinness had examined every tiny detail of Dublin's style of play, from Stephen Cluxton's kick outs, to Bernard Brogan or whoever got in a shot at goal at the other end of the field. He had them mapped like something a doctor might find in a CT scan.

Jim called it 'tracking' them.

Starting with Stephen Cluxton.

He had hours and hours of DVDs of Cluxton kicking the ball out. He had studied them religiously, but he did admit that he was finding it difficult to actually decipher a pattern.

He concluded that Cluxton was just too good with his kicks. If there was something almost scientific at work, McGuinness, despite pouring over those DVDs, could not see it. His only conclusion was that perhaps Cluxton was simply going through his lines, looking for one of his full backs and if any of them was free he'd chip the ball out. If not, he would hit someone on the half back line. If not, he'd go to the next line, Cian O'Sullivan or Michael Darragh Macauley, or see if Paul Flynn was an option. The primary ball receivers however were Diarmuid Connolly, Flynn and O'Sullivan.

We knew, once Dublin got the ball away, that ninety-nine per cent of their scores came from within an arc in front of the opponent's goal. That arc was 50 metres long on the end line and reached out to the 45 metres line.

McGuinness told us that everything outside of this arc did not matter. He told us to defend the arc only. If Dublin had a ball outside the arc then there was no need to chase it down.

All we had to do was to defend our arc. And in front of Papa, or Paul Durcan in our goals, we had 12 men at all times defending. Always, a minimum of 12 men. McGuinness had all of the Dublin stats. He had maps of them, and numbers! He had every shot they had ever taken in the 2014 championship. Every score they got. He showed it all to us every single evening before training.

'Defend that zone with your f****** life!'

That was the order.

After that, well, according to McGuinness, after that the winning of the game was going to be easy.

He worked out that 'easy' bit for us as well.

'It's bullshit… all bullshit, boys!' he kept telling us. 'It's the journalists and the media… they're making Dublin this team nobody can beat.'

In real life, McGuinness also wanted us to put Bernard Brogan, and whoever else was ending up in Dublin's full forward line, under the most intense pressure they had ever experienced in their lives. So massively intense, and constant every time the ball came anywhere near him, that Brogan and the others would break down.

Physically and mentally, our pressure was designed to break each of them down completely.

Rid Brogan of his composure.

Tear away his first layer, and then his second layer, of confidence. And leave him bare, and panicky.

If Brogan or anyone else managed to get a kick in, inside the arc, then they would be doing so looking more like a snivelling wreck of a forward rather than the beautifully balanced and certain forward he looked in every game he had played in 2014 before then.

Better still, McGuinness wanted Dublin shooting outside of their favourite scoring zone, outside of their comfort zone, far outside of the arc we had placed on the field.

'Put them in a pressure place... a place they have never prepared themselves for in their lives!' That was the directive.

We were not to let up on Brogan or Diarmuid Connolly or Paul Flynn, or anyone else. The Dublin free takers, Brogan and Connolly, had to be hounded and badgered twice as much, three times as much as any other player. Break the pair of them down, mentally and physically!

That was it.

And when Dublin won a free, and the time came for Brogan or Connolly to step up and ready themselves, the job was to ensure that during that brief moment of calm, each of them would have trouble remembering their own names after what they had been experiencing. Never mind recalculating the simple act of kicking the ball over the bar.

'Break them down...!'

To win the game ourselves, we had to win the ball back.

McGuinness had always warned us to give the opposition no time on the ball. That warning came early in 2011. He wanted intensity in every tackle and he wanted multiple tackles being made on every man who came anywhere near our 45 metres line with the ball. He did not mind if I sprinted at a man, bought a dummy solo and landed on the flat of my back, looking a bit of a fool.

McGuinness was happy enough with that.

That was tackle number one, in McGuinness' book.

He did not mind if the first tackle went astray at all, because he knew there would be a second tackle coming in that very same second. And the man who had just defied one tackle was going to have to get his head together and deal with another tackle. And another tackle after that. And another one.

'What's that man going to be doing... when he's dodging you if you are the first tackler?

'What's he going to be thinking?' McGuinness would ask.

'He's not thinking about scoring!' McGuinness would also answer.

'All he's thinking is getting the f*** out of the way of this maniac charging at him... that's what he's... THINKING!'

McGuinness promised us that footballers become overwhelmed within seconds, that they can not process that sort of pressure. All that man's brain is telling him... ORDERING him, is to get to hell out of the way of the tackle. And when a second tackle and a third tackle comes in, the man is blotting out every single thought he ever had about scoring. Or even passing the ball. He just wants to hold onto the ball. He's ORDERING himself again. But then the man starts to panic. He stops thinking altogether. He decides to try to get rid of the ball before he loses it.

Usually, at that point, it is not difficult to take the ball from that same man's arms. Job done. Ball safely back where it belongs.

Though it was not all that simple.

The bedrock of getting that ball back was to get back into defence, work like an absolute dog, make contact with the man, take lumps out of him, and continue tackling like a maniac. Every single time we lost the ball.

Always make contact.

'Contact... contact!' was the order in training every second minute. In training every single night Jim and Rory would never stop with their orders.

'Thump him... thump him...

'...THUMP HIM... WILL YA!'

Every second minute. Every night at training.

Religiously.

Always with an animalistic intent. He wanted our tackling to be ravenous, and he wanted the man on the ball to know we were taking bites out of him.

'THUMP HIM...

'THUMP... HIM...

'WILL YOU F******... THUMP HIM!'

In small, four-sided games we learned to thump one another like we intended thumping our opponents the next Sunday. There were two small nets at either end. The space was tight and confined. The ball was thrown in and every time a team scored, those four men could leave the field.

The four other sorry souls stayed put.

Four new men came in immediately, and the ball was thrown in again. The shouting would start.

'THUMP HIM... THUMP...

'THUMP...

'... HIM...'

We would be there, thumping the living daylights out of one another for 30, 40 seconds, until someone got free and got the ball into the net. Another four men would race in.

'THUMP HIM... THUMP HIM!'

It was horrific for four men if they had to stay on the field for three or four games in a row, but if they did, they would be subjected to ever increasing demands to fight their way out of their misery.

'THUMP HIM.... THUMP HIM...

'YOU'VE GOT TO F****** ...

'... THUMP HIM!'

There were five years between me and my older brother, Barry. He was a Manchester United fan. My four sisters all supported Liverpool. And they won me over. I had my Liverpool Candy strip, home and away, and I could be anybody on any particular day out on the park near our house... Barnes, Peter Beardsley, Ian Rush, but I also had my Magee Donegal strip and, in a flick of a switch, I could also be Tony Boyle or Barry McGowan.

Living my dreams in the best of both worlds.

In Scoil Cholmcille, where I now teach, Tom Redden was the principal and he was big into his football. He was a Derryman. Football came first, soccer second. My sisters played a lot of football with St Eunan's, and Barry too, until one day he was climbing a big cast iron gate which fell on him and damaged his leg. He preferred his golf mostly after that. The gate could have killed him. Not long after that we were playing soccer on the park with our next door neighbours, the McClaffertys, seven of them, all boys, and Barry broke his leg again.

I went to the club most Sunday mornings for coaching, but I was also playing as much soccer as I could every day. That's all I wanted to do, play football and soccer.

On soccer teams I was getting to travel everywhere. I wore the green and gold stripes of Ballyraine managed by John O'Doherty, then the white and black colours of Letterkenny and District Schoolboys, then the green and gold of Donegal Schoolboys.

We won Ulster titles, fought for All-Irelands, and travelled all over, down to Dublin, Waterford, Cork. Charlie Shiels and Andy O'Boyle and their helpers treated us like kings, like we were playing for Liverpool. They were great men and gave us a tremendous footballing education.

Cathal Greene, Mickey Gibbons and Martin Rafferty, Kevin's late father, never had a problem with that, but they wanted St Eunan's to come first. Wearing the black and amber of St Eunan's was special to me though. And it was with St Eunan's that I also suffered my first heartbreak.

A few days before the Under-10 county final I came to a nasty ending in Gortlee Forest beside our housing estate. The McClaffertys and myself were taking turns clinging to a big swooping branch and looking to hold onto this branch, as though it was a wild bull, while the other boys pulled it back as far as they could like a catapult.

I was sent flying and clattered into another tree and broke my wrist. In the county final I wore my cast. I got a new cast on especially for the game, thanks to my mother's friends in the hospital. I got a glove over the cast and I lined out centre-forward. But I could only use one hand. I was standing around the place and watching us lose.

A total of 7,385 people paid into MacCumhaill Park to see us take on Antrim in the preliminary round of the championship, but their manager, Liam Bradley said after the game that if he had been asked to put his hand into his pocket to get into the ground he would have refused, and hightailed it home. It was safe to say he didn't like what he saw out there on the field.

I can't say I enjoyed it much myself.

The attendance was 5,000 less than the number who had turned up to see Antrim beat us in Ballybofey two years earlier. It's true, the game was not nice to look at it. We were operating McGuinness' system for the first time in the championship, but we were far from clinical. The ball spilled from first to last during the 70 minutes. It was the proverbial bar of soap, and passes were going astray from the boot too. Passes were also being wasted from the hand.

Antrim knew what was facing them, and they sat back as well.

It was a strange afternoon.

We could all sense, almost feel the weight of the pressure. It was daunting. I could actually feel the impatience and the fears of our own supporters bearing down upon us. It was like the 'want' of our own supporters was sweeping down upon the field.

It was a game we could not lose.

Lose... and where could we go?

After 20 minutes it was still level, 0-1 each. Kevin Niblock equalised for them after Colm McFadden had opened the scoring with a free. We were simply scared.

I didn't want to go forward. I was choosing to stay back, even though my orders were to go forward every time we got the ball, to get ahead of the man on the ball and provide options.

That was fine in theory, and it was a theory I had bought into, but out on the field my legs were heavy, my lungs were heaving. I was telling myself to go forward, but then I was fighting with myself to stay back.

It was safer to stay.

I knew Jim McGuinness wouldn't be happy at half time, but there were so many turnovers happening in the middle of the field and what if I was tearing up the field and there was a breakdown and my man had a free run at Papa in our goals?

What would McGuinness have to say to me then?

It wasn't just me. I could see the fear in the faces all around me. I had started in the middle of the field with Martin McElhinney. Big Neil didn't get his game and wasn't brought in.

In the last 15 minutes before half time, we inched forward a little more. Ryan Bradley kicked two good points and that calmed us. Adrian Hanlon, Dermot Molloy and Murph also had points by half time. It was 0-6 to 0-3. Nobody was happy back in the dressing room.

Murph continued to play deep, right back in the middle of the field in the second half. People were going to have a lot to say about that in the week that followed also. At a quick glance, it looked like madness.

Michael Murphy doing household chores on the field when he should have been readying himself inside for his supply of the ball? He finished the day with three points from frees, and that was never going to be enough to halt the grumbling of some supporters.

On a more positive note for Donegal folk, they got to see Paddy McBrearty play his first few minutes of senior championship football. Those who paid in got double value for money, in fact, because Paddy scored 1-3 in the minor game, and then was sent into our game after 53 minutes. Paddy was 17 years-old and was next in line, after Murph, a real prodigy, the next Great White Hope for Donegal football.

I knew him from club football, and I knew he was quick and strong on the ball. But I was surprised to see him being brought in. He looked at home once he got the first ball into his hands, but, strangely, he wasn't wearing gloves. We soon learned that he did not like wearing gloves. He used red Dax Wax instead!

Gloves stopped him from getting a feel for the ball in his hands. And even if it was bucketing down, he'd refuse to get himself a pair. Though Jim McGuinness did have a word with him about that after the game. Paddy eventually went out and bought himself his first pair of gloves.

Tomas McCann got a point for them straight after the break. That was a kick up the backside for us, and it worked and we took the next four scores. It was 0-10 to 0-4 when Neil McGee had to throw himself at full stretch to block a sure goal chance from Niblock. If that had gone in we'd have been fighting for our lives in the last 10 minutes, and I'm not entirely sure how we would have coped if we had to urgently wrap the game up in a reckless finish.

Instead, Kevin Rafferty set up Mark McHugh for a goal, and McHugh allowed their goalkeeper to commit himself before rifling the ball into the back of the net. 1-10 to 0-7 was how it finished, and in the Villa Rose Hotel afterwards, once we had eaten our dinner, McGuinness stood up and congratulated us on our victory.

There was no big smile on his face.

We all felt relieved.

He just looked sombre. We had done the job for him, badly, but it was done and over with just the same.

We had won a championship game in Ulster for the first time in four years. We were now in the first round. He told us it would be like this, that people would be critical of our style. All that matters though are the results, he assured us.

We were still starting from scratch.

CHAPTER 3

Early in 2011, with Antrim beaten, and the first round of the Ulster championship awaiting us three weeks later, McGuinness was in foul mood. The 'Man of the Match' award versus Antrim had reluctantly been given out to Ryan Bradley on *The Sunday Game*.

He was the best of a bad lot, they said.

The game, they also claimed, was the worst game of football they had ever seen.

They had always liked to poke at us. Like we were furry animals in a zoo who would never bite back.

Telling us we were too soft. We were too nice.

And now, they were telling us that we were making a mockery of the game of Gaelic football with our great, big, fattened defence.

'Bollix!.... Pure Bollix!' Jim told us, often enough.

He told us we knew exactly what we were doing.

'We're going to an Ulster final!' he promised us. And once there, once we got to Clones on the day of the Ulster final, he promised us we'd have a second medal in our pockets.

Tyrone and Armagh didn't need anyone in a newspaper to tell them that we were soft. The two of them knew that to be a fact.

They knew we would not stand up.

They one hundred per cent believed that.

Armagh especially. Even when they had only beaten us by a goal in the Ulster final in Croke Park, in 2006, they made sure to let us know what they thought of us. Brian McIver was leaving their dressing room after congratulating them on their win when he heard someone tell him that he would never win anything with a bunch of cubs.

Brian was fuming when he got back to us.

But it was Tyrone who interested Jim McGuinness more. Tyrone was Jim's yardstick, not Armagh. It was Tyrone who won three All-Irelands, he reminded us. Tyrone won all the big battles with the whole country watching. Tyrone were the greatest team in Ireland for a full decade.

Jim wanted Tyrone.

Armagh were gone. They were finished, he told us. Armagh were old hat, whereas there was still life in Tyrone. Just enough life to make them dangerous, but Jim told us we were stronger than them. We were fitter and faster than them.

Tyrone were further down the road.

We played Cavan on a dirty, wet, miserable Sunday afternoon in June in the first round of the championship. It was like a winter's day in Breffni Park. I was in the middle of the field with Kevin Rafferty. Big Neil wasn't thrown in until the 58th minute when the game was long over. It was actually over 10 minutes or so before he came on, when we were already six points up, when Colm McFadden won the ball inside and saw me racing from deep, alone, my man stranded far behind me, and laid the ball off perfectly.

I pulled the trigger 15, 16 yards out, low and hard, and found the bottom corner. 2-8 to 0-3. That was the end of Cavan.

When we walked into the Radisson Blu Hotel in Cavan we had quickly discovered that we had a 20 minutes wait until our pre-match meal was ready.

We were doing some light stretching on the floor to loosen up after the bus journey. We were all busy chatting to one another, passing the time.

JD McGrenra was our physical therapist and Pat Shovelin was our goalkeeping coach. Jim ordered the two of them to close all of the curtains in this enormous room that was vacant of any tables or chairs. I wondered what was going on?

'Ok ... lights off!' Jim ordered.

'We have 15 minutes until our meal is ready.

'Close the eyes... and get some rest!'

So the lights went out.

The room went into complete darkness. You couldn't see the man lying next to you.

I was lying there on the carpet along with the rest of the squad with my eyes closed and thinking this is bizarre. In a few hours we are going to war with Cavan, but at this moment in time we are being asked to close our eyes and go to sleep.

It was all too easy. Cavan put up a fight alright, but they didn't play much football. They were mostly cranky and looking for trouble. And with Karl Lacey not giving their talisman, Seanie Johnston a sniff of the ball, their frustration grew and grew.

We had a date with Tyrone in the Ulster semi-final.

McGuinness was cranky as well after the game. He told reporters that he was fed up with Donegal, the whole damned county, being disrespected. He told us he was fed up with the laughing and the sneering.

As for Tyrone?

He told reporters that we had no chance of beating them unless he saw a vast improvement.

Three weeks later, at half time in Clones, I was sitting in the dressing room and I was getting a roasting from McGuinness in front of everybody. Tyrone were leading by two points, 0-6 to 0-4. It was hot and difficult to fill the lungs with the humidity. It was overpowering for the first 10 minutes of the game. Clones is one of those grounds which seems dug deep into the earth. Some days the heat can simply roll down the hills and down from the stand and devour you. Your lungs can burn up faster in Clones than anywhere else in Ireland. But McGuinness was more concerned with our stupidity, not the humidity.

It was our first Ulster semi final in five years.

He had told us what to do. He had ordered me exactly what to do. But we were all gasping for air, we were not getting our defensive shape, we were running after Tyrone men, we were not retreating back to our lines when they had the ball. I was running after this man and that man. I had no idea where I was running half the time. My head was gone. No system was being applied by us as a team. Nobody was thinking.

Boys with numbers 8 and 9, 10, 11 and 12 had to *think* to make our system work. They had to think all the time, and never forget what they had to do when we lost the ball. We needed to sprint back and get our shape every single time. When we are not *thinking*, when we are not doing our jobs, there is no system.

Tyrone were running through us. They should have been further in front. It might have been lights out by the time we got back into the dressing room at half time.

McGuinness had also ordered me to go man to man with Sean Cavanagh in the first half. But Tyrone did not let that happen.

I should have made it happen.

I wanted to mark Cavanagh, but Kevin Hughes wanted to mark me. There was all of this sorting out to be done, and no football was being played. Every time I went to get to Cavanagh, Hub Hughes walked across me. He and I had spent the first 10 minutes, 15 minutes, pushing and dunting one another. He was holding my shirt. He was telling me that I was going nowhere and that he was staying with me the whole game.

I had been yellow carded after five minutes. The ball had been played to the on rushing Sean Cavanagh somewhere near the 21 metre line. He had a clear run on goal with only Papa to beat. I couldn't take the risk of letting him get the shot off so I pulled him back and took the yellow card.

Concession of a point was better than a goal, even though I had to play the rest of the game with a yellow card. Looking back now that was a good foul to give away, as a goal might have buried us. Hughes would be yellow carded in the 60th and 62nd minutes, and that was the end of him for the day.

The game was 16 minutes in when Paddy McBrearty kicked over our first point. Kevin Rafferty hit our second in the 30th minute. After the game, Mickey Harte counted out 18 scoring chances they had in the opening half. In comparison, we had five chances. They should also have kicked the first goal of the game when Stephen O'Neill had a great opportunity. Anthony Thompson though got back and made a vital block to keep us in the game. It was a huge moment. Tony had given away possession originally but did brilliantly to atone for his error.

'I gave you instructions before the game... didn't I?'

McGuinness was not looking for me to reply to his question at half time. It was not a conversation.

'I told you what to do... and you haven't f****** done it, have you?'

'HAVE YOU?'

He was standing in the middle of the room, and he was mad as hell.

'You need to f****** sort it out!'

His words felt like a kick in the teeth.

'Sort it out... Rory!' McGuinness demanded.

'What the f*** are you doing?

'Why the f*** are you not running back into defence?' he asked .

The game was half over and McGuinness had seen nothing good from me.

He had told all of us how we would beat Tyrone.

He had been telling us since the start of the year. It was all Tyrone, Tyrone... Tyrone! He had never stopped talking about Tyrone. At times it seemed they were the only team he was interested in talking about. In the three weeks after we had beaten Cavan, every night in training... Tyrone, Tyrone... Tyrone!

They need to be broken down, he told us.

They need to be stopped running down the middle, he told us.

Beating Tyrone will define us, he told us.

Or losing to Tyrone will leave us nowhere, he told us.

The night before the game, in the Slieve Russell Hotel, we'd had our craic and banter, we'd stretched in the pool, we had tried our best to loosen up over the dinner table with some relaxed banter, and then we'd done our tactical work. One last hour and a half of Tyrone, and then to bed, 11.30 pm and a goodnight to Big Neil who would not see one minute of the action the next day. The next morning breakfast was taken as quickly as possible, and more Tyrone. Everyone knew what they had to do. Every inch of the Tyrone team had been covered. Inside and out.

We were prepared for the verbals too.

We had been warned not to get involved with the Ricey McMenamins, the Doohers, the Gormleys or whoever else wanted to start some sledging.

Look them in the eye and say .... 'not today'

'NOT TODAY RYAN......

'NOT TODAY BRIAN!'

Look them in the eye... smile, and give them the line.

I remember back in 2007, Tyrone were well on their way to eliminating us from the Ulster Championship in Clones at the semi final stage. Colm McFadden had been blown up for over carrying the ball on the edge of the Tyrone D with time slipping away. He was surrounded by Tyrone players. Not content with winning the free and winning the game, Brian Dooher grabbed the ball and proceeded to roar into Colm's face.

'YESSSSSSS! ...COME ON!'

Colm took the bait and plugged him with a little uppercut under the chin. Dooher went down holding his face and Colm got his marching orders.

We were warned not to get involved this time around.

'Are you going to do what you were asked to do, Rory?

'Are you going to go out there... and do it?'

It still was not a conversation.

I nodded my head.

Grunted.

Michael Murphy kicked a point two minutes into the second-half. That was important. In the second half we remembered everything we had ever been told about Tyrone by McGuinness. Every last thing. We started to break the ball with conviction on their kickouts and we were picking up the breaks. By the end of the game we had them running in circles when they had the ball, and looking for room down the left sideline, down the right sideline.

We also began to find Murph and Colm up front. And midway through the half we took the lead. Michael Hegarty sent a direct pass into Murph who swivelled. He fisted a long pass to Karlo who had kept running ahead. Karlo gave it to McFadden. Colm faked to shoot with his left and switched to his right, his wrong foot. He still rifled his shot past Pascal McConnell. 1-6 to 0-9. Colm McFadden always loved to score goals with his right foot. In training, a right footed goal was twice as satisfying to him as a left footed goal.

The scoreline at the finish looked like a 'get out of jail' win alright, but we knew how we would get out of jail.

It all came flooding back after that goal. Then Murph clattered Ryan McMenamin as he came out with the ball. He found Dermot Molloy who'd just come into the game.

'Put it over... put the f****** thing over!'

I was 40 yards down the field, but I was still roaring at Molloy.

He whacked it to the back of the net.

Two goals and six points.

That was our lot for the day. Tyrone scored nine points. We won by getting back into defence, all of us in the middle. That was our platform to launch a counter attack. Breaking up their attacks and supporting the man on the ball with aggressive running from the back.

That's what McGuinness had ordered at half time.

Every time we lost the ball, we moved back and got our shape. Every time, I was back at the top of the D in front of our goalmouth. Every single time. Every time, instinctively, I was there. Where I needed to be, where I was told to be. I stopped chasing runners. Instead, I stopped them running down the middle. And I tackled like a dog.

But Jim McGuinness said we were missing something. We lacked composure, he told us. He wanted us composed and tackling like rabid dogs, like mad men. That's what he wanted in the Ulster final.

It was going to be the first Ulster final in 13 years without either Tyrone or Armagh defending the Anglo Celt Cup. They had taken the last dozen titles home, one or other of them. It was Derry who last won an Ulster title, before that, back in 1998 when Joe Brolly was blowing kisses to the Donegal support.

Donegal had not been in a final since 2006, the year I finally won a starting place on the team after four years.

On July 18, 2011, Jim McGuinness put a second medal, in addition to the league Division Two medal, into our pockets. Donegal beat Derry 1-11 to 0-8. It was our first Ulster title since 1992.

And only Donegal's sixth since the beginning of time.

My left ankle was giving me bother again during the 2011 season. I was getting pain every time I planted my foot to jump or sprint. In the lead up to the 2011 Ulster final, I knew I was in trouble. Deep down I knew, although if I talked with anyone, I told them the ankle was fine.

'No problem!' I said, '.. it's coming along well.'

I would tell that to physios, friends, family. It didn't matter. Even Jim and Rory were told the same thing.

Jim gave me nearly two weeks to get it right after the Tyrone game but insisted that I take full part in training in O'Donnell Park the week of the game. So that was my goal. To run out on the pitch on the Tuesday evening and look comfortable and pain free.

I have to get through this session, I thought to myself.

I knew it would be a short, intensive session. The warm up was fine, the kicking afterwards also fine. Then it was into a truck and trailer drill at around sixty percent. No problem.

'Ok boys.. now flat out for 90 seconds!'

'Everything you have!' was the order from Jim.

I was in discomfort but I never let on. I kept going. Desperate to get through the drill and onto the next phase of training. *I am fine*, I kept repeating to myself in my mind, but my ankle was throbbing.

We then went into some short sided games.

Get it... give it... nothing mad, I told myself.

No need to be a hero.

We played seven minute games. Four or five of them. I managed to get through each one without overly exerting myself. I avoided jumping altogether. It was a good job all restarts were short from the 'keepers. I got through the session and in my head it was mission accomplished.

I still had doubts that I looked convincing enough for Jim and Rory to pick me in the middle of the park.

'How did it feel?' they asked afterwards. 'Any pain?'

'No .. it's grand, not too bad at all.'

'That's good Rory,' replied McGuinness, '... you have four more days now.

Jim McGuinness, that Tuesday night in Letterkenny, knew I wasn't fully fit to face Derry. But he also knew how desperate I was to play in the final. He could see it in my eyes. He knew the work that I put in all year, the good league campaign I put in and, I suppose, he wanted to repay me with a starting place in the final. He granted me my wish and named me at number eight.

I lasted just over half an hour before coming off. It was pure adrenalin that kept me going even for that long. My ankle simply wasn't strong enough.

It looked like Brian McIver had 'SAVIOUR' written on the back of his bib, not 'BAINISTEOIR'. It also looked like he knew exactly what he was doing.

From the earliest weeks of his reign, in the McKenna Cup and league, he was naming me on his starting fifteen.

Almost everything went right in 2006.

We had the usual problems, of course. Every year, someone and his mate broke ranks and were usually, but not always, thrown off the panel for indiscipline.

Indiscipline.

That was the word that people around the country most associated with the Donegal football team. And every year, like waiting for a clock to chime midnight, they would not be one bit surprised when it was announced in the small print in newspapers that so-and-so from Donegal, or so-and-so and a couple of others, had been told to go home and to stay home for the year.

Indiscipline in Donegal meant drinking.

Nothing else. Indiscipline meant that someone had acted the eejit, and stayed drinking in a pub in his local town on a night when it had been agreed that nobody would drink. Sometimes, boys would be complete fools. They would stay drinking, miss a training session, and work their way around a few pubs in their town. Just to make sure that everyone and his mother got word what they were doing.

There was a madness to it.

And in 2007, I was one of those eejits. I went for a few drinks on a Tuesday night, a training night, without a thought in the world about the man who had finally shown complete faith in me and named me on his starting team.

That's how I thanked Brian McIver in 2007.

Exactly 12 months earlier, in the spring of 2006, as we were preparing to play Louth in the Division Two league final, it was Kevin Cassidy and Eamon McGee who decided they needed a few drinks. They were told to leave the panel immediately by McIver.

A month earlier, on Paddy's Day, he had decided to go for one pint on the Friday, a visit which turned into a massive session.

We were due to play Clare on the Sunday and he missed the bus. So what does he decide to do? Eamon jumps into a taxi and tells the driver to take him to Carlow. He leaves Donegal for Carlow.

He also rings Brian McIver.

'Jesus… Eamon, we're down in Clare here!' McIver tells him. So Eamon cuts across the country and lands in Galway.

The taxi actually left him off in a pub where there was a traveller's funeral going on. But he got one of his mates in Galway to pick him up and drop him down to Clare.

He landed at the hotel steaming. Cass had to put him to bed. It was crazy business though, as Eamon says himself… 'that was the mild stuff!'

With or without Eamon and Cass in 2006, we thought we were too good for Louth. The game ended in a draw after they made a wild comeback. We still thought we had a divine right to beat Louth.

We lost the replay.

One month later, I was named to start a championship game for the first time, on the right wing. We had Down at home in MacCumhaill Park. I had travelled to Belfast with Kathryn's father, John on the Monday before the game. The management had arranged for me to get an injection for a troublesome hip flexor.

I went to the Musgrave Park Hospital for the procedure. I remember the feeling of dread coming over me as I watched the doctor produce this huge needle!

I hate needles.

He was going to go in at the side of my right hip and he was using an ultrasound machine to guide himself to the correct muscle.

'Couldn't you knock me out first?' I asked.

He laughed and said, 'don't worry... you ll be fine'.

I wasn't joking. I really wished he would knock me out. That needle must have been 8 or 10 centimetres long. I nearly passed out when I saw it.

'You will feel a slight nip now as I go into the muscle,' he said.

I was glad to get out of there and my feelings towards needles were ten times worse after that experience. He told me to do nothing for 48 hours. No training, no driving, careful going up and down stairs, etc, etc. I took part in training with the team on the Thursday and the hip flexor felt great. The injection had been a success and I was ready to go.

We beat Down by one point, 1-12 to 1-11, and I scored the goal of my life. I actually scored one goal and two points. And in my second championship start against Derry in the Ulster semi final, I scored five points, all of them from play. We also beat Derry by five points, 1-13 to 0-11, in Clones. We were a young team and we were through to the Ulster final to meet Armagh in Croke Park.

Eamon McGee was back in McIver's good books and starting again. But Brendan Devenney had decided to take a break and play some soccer. And Cass had kept walking when he was shown the door and ended up spending the summer in Boston.

As far as I was concerned, the past seemed like some sort of old history book which had been left up high on some shelf. Who cared about 2005 or 2004, or any year before the summer of 2006?

My goal against Down had everyone talking. It was one of those one in a thousand goals, I'll admit. Big Neil had fetched it in the middle. He gave it to Michael Hegarty who passed the ball to Barry Dunnion, and I was coming up on his shoulder. He popped it to me.

The whole Down defence parted in front of me.

I was going through at some pace.

I'll drive this hard over the bar, I thought to myself. When I looked at the goal that night on the television I could see myself hesitating, slightly breaking my stride, but then driving on another two or three yards.

I hit it crisply.

Top right hand corner of the net.

I had my first point with my left foot, the second with my right.

Then I got the goal.

If first championship games come in the form of dreams, I might as well have been sleeping the most contented sleep of my life.

I knew I had to play well. Too many people had been looking at me playing league games and bits of championship games, and sitting on the bench for too long. I had been waiting for four years, and I knew that if I did not make an impact it would be only human nature for most supporters around the county to think to themselves that I simply did not have what was needed.

After four years I was not going to have supporters patiently waiting for me to come good in the big games.

Back home in the town, in Gallagher's Hotel, my whole family were waiting for me after we had beaten Down. I got in the door just as The Sunday Game was coming on. My mother and father were there, my brother and all my sisters. Everyone from the club seemed to be there.

I was given a seat in the middle of the main bar.

Sitting next to me was Mickey 'Boy' O'Donnell, one of the great GAA men in Letterkenny. He was a great character in our club and in our town. He never stopped working for the good of St Eunan's. He was our kit man for years and years, God rest him. At the time he was our club president.

He was wearing his St Eunan's black jacket with the club's emblem on the breast pocket. He was proud as punch, I could see. And I was so damned happy to have done my club proud.

We all waited for the goal.

Then came a big cheer, and Mickey grabbed my shoulders and shook me with delight.

Life could not have been any better.

● ● ●

Around the corner was the 2006 Ulster final in Croke Park.

Around the same corner was Armagh.

We were on a roll. We had a young team, and seven of us would be playing in Croke Park for the first time. We were also looking to win three championship games in a row. Whereas, Armagh were aiming for three Ulster titles in a row. At the time, lucky enough, we did not know the difference.

We would have been better off playing Armagh in Clones. Croke Park was too big for us, too far a climb mentally. In Croke Park, we needed everything to go exactly right for us and everyone needed to play well. Armagh, on the other hand, knew how to win games there, whether they were on the boil or not.

They did not play all that well in the Ulster final in 2006, but they still won, 1-9 to 0-9. Only one goal stood between us, but in reality the difference between the final and my first two championship games for Donegal was like day and night. Against Down I had space. Against Derry, who were not man-marking, I had the freedom of the pitch, moving into the corner, moving back out to the half line, with nobody laying a hand on me.

Andy Mallon was a whole different proposition.

From the first minute of the Ulster final, it was clear that he loved what he had to do. He was at my side every second. He was breathing down my back, he was holding my arm, he was as close as he could get without being inside my shirt.

I could not take a breath without Andy Mallon checking what I was up to? Once, I had escaped from his grasp and managed to slip the ball over the bar but that was about it for 70 minutes. I had never met a marker as tight.

It was more than a game of football. It was a ball game alright, but there were a whole lot of other games also wrapped up in the 70 minutes. Games I barely understood.

Armagh, technically, won their sixth Ulster title in eight years because of Paul McGrane's goal, a real thunderbolt just after half time. After that we were chasing them, but they were never in any real danger of being caught. Stephen McDermott ghosted inside their full back line one minute into added time, but his shot, like our whole performance over the afternoon, was calmly enough deflected away by Paul Hearty in their goals.

We were brave, and none more so than Christy Toye, Eamon McGee, Karl Lacey, Barry Dunnion and Barry Monaghan. Karlo did one of his inch perfect displays and kept McDonnell so very quiet. However, they had Kieran McGeeney who controlled them at the back. John McEntee hammered over two points with his usual ease from far out. And then McGrane nailed us in the 37th minute. They were cynical, aggressive, sickeningly assured right to the very end.

But McIver had chosen to go with youth in his first year in charge, and a one goal defeat by Armagh spelled some promise. A win over Fermanagh in round four of the qualifiers followed. Again, I had a man marker for the day and their manager, my own clubmate Charlie Mulgrew, knew full well what to expect from me. The summer then came to a halt with a single point defeat by Cork in the All-Ireland quarter final, which seemed like a more than decent return in Brian McIver's first year.

We had started well against Cork. I had a freshness return to my legs, and had a point to my name when I got a knee into my back. One of their big men in the middle of the field did the damage, Murphy or O'Neill, or was it Kavanagh? I never found out who it was. I broke two ribs. After 54 minutes I was on the sideline struggling to breathe.

On the bus, on the way home, I was still struggling. Every bump on the route left me wanting to howl.

But I kept as quiet as I could. I had been bandaged up in the dressing room, and there was an ice pack tied to my back. I just wanted to get home.

Home, and then get out. Not to the hospital. That could wait until the next morning, because there was a first season as a Donegal footballer, a fully fledged Donegal footballer to be celebrated, and I wanted to start right away.

Two days later, I headed up to the hospital in town for my x-rays.

Every night, on McGuinness' list of 20 key performance indicators, is 'shot selection'. Good possession means nothing unless the right shot at goals is selected at the end of every movement up the field. McGuinness talked about shot selection all of the time, and by the middle of 2012 we became very good at it. We became a very unselfish team. More often than not the player in the best position would get the ball.

'I don't give a f*** who puts the ball over the bar!

'Not one f***!

'The ball will find the solution.

'Keep it moving... the ball will work itself out.'

McGuinness stressed this to us every night at training. Our conversion rate had us the No.1 team in the country at making possession count. That's what McGuinness told us, and he also showed us sheets of statistics that proved we were the No.1 team in the country, no doubt about it. Or so he said!

Whether it was true or not, Jim McGuinness wanted us to believe that there was no other team better than Donegal at selecting the right shot.

In the 2011 Ulster final we had still selected our shots pretty well. We could do better, of course. McGuinness knew that, but he also saw in that game that the essential difference between us and Derry was having enough composure and sufficient wit to decide as a team who should shoot at goal, and from where?

Derry's return from 22 scoring chances was eight points, and that was not good enough, not nearly good enough.

It worked out at around a 36% success rate. We normally operated at around 60% conversion rate. The stats were in our favour and we were confident that if we implemented our gameplan we wouldn't be beaten. It also helped that we held them scoreless for 21 minutes. That sort of long wait for a score leaves a team frantic. Composure during a lengthy spell such as that goes right out the window.

They were two good reasons why we won. The third was Michael Murphy's goal which came from a soft penalty decision. It came two minutes into the second half when we were level, 0-5 apiece. Murph chased a long ball sent in by Michael Hegarty. Their goalkeeper, Danny Devlin rushed out to meet him. As the ball sailed wide, Devlin's tackle brought down Murph.

Fourteen months beforehand, McGuinness's Under-21s had trailed Dublin by two points in the All-Ireland final when Cillian Morrison won a penalty two minutes from time. With every eye in Breffni Park upon him, Murph took responsibility. His kick rattled the crossbar, hitting it so hard it almost landed back out at the 45. Jim Gavin's Dublin won, 1-10 to 1-8.

Murph, though, wasn't one for shirking responsibility. He thundered the ball to the net this time. In the next few minutes he laid off scores for Colm McFadden to his left, and Hegarty to his right. We were five points in front. We sailed home.

But it took hard work all the same. Defending a lead had become ingrained in us by the middle of McGuinness' first summer. We'd get better at it, but even in 2011 we started to take delight, and gain real satisfaction in defending.

We refused to let our core defence be breached. We were not yet masters at closing out games, but we were getting clinical enough. We broke up Derry attack after attack, and then countered.

Each time we got the ball to the right man in enough space. Each time Derry got the ball they faced second, third and fourth phase tackling and, inevitably, as we knew it would, their ball was spilled.

With each spill there was a huge surging roar from the crowd. It was the same roar that had sickened me as we were losing the 2005 Donegal final to McGuinness' Glenties. Now that roar energised us. We loved that roar.

It was like more of a standing ovation.

It told us that our hard work was simply outstanding.

Throughout that second half, I was sitting on the side of the pitch. I was watching our boys tackling. Then I'd hear a roar, and the ground would be raised off its feet. I had hobbled out of the game after 33 minutes. Big Neil and myself had started in the middle of the field, as Kevin Rafferty was injured, and we finished with Big Neil and Martin McElhinney dominating in the middle third. Big Neil was magnificent. His fielding was inspiring, and drew roars of approval from the crowd all on their own.

Watching, Jim McGuinness understood that Big Neil might have a serious role to play on the team. I could see that too, and I knew that I would have a fight on my hands to nail down my own starting place.

We had all gone back to play a round of club championships after beating Tyrone in the semi final. There had been a lot of talk about it. McGuinness knew better than anyone how precious Ulster titles were, and how difficult it was to win one. He had done that in 1992 on Brian McEniff's team, but in the 19 years wait after that he had also lost Ulster finals in 1993, 1998, 2002 and 2004. Jim McGuinness had a giant craving for Ulster titles every year, and when he regained the provincial crown in 2014, after losing it to Monaghan a year earlier, some people were amazed at his excitement and manic reaction on the pitch immediately after the game.

But, to Jim, an Ulster title was pure gold.

He did not want us playing any club games before the 2011 Ulster final. He did not get his way that summer but after that, he won the argument and ensured that the County Board never again tried to squeeze a round of club games into pockets of the summer. He cleared the entire summer out in future.

I was off.

Gone.

Sitting on the sideline.

Watching and listening.

Waiting for the final whistle.

I was overjoyed, and I tried to run out onto the field when the referee blew his whistle for the last time, using my good leg like a pogo stick. Then I decided to run on both legs. There was, suddenly, inexplicably, no pain worth talking about. My ankle was in bits, and it would be thumping with pain all night and the following morning, but out on the field in the minutes after the Ulster final had ended, as I chased after my teammates and we danced together, I simply didn't care.

We were Ulster champions. We were in the All-Ireland quarter-final. However, I wondered if my summer was over?

CHAPTER 4

Winning the All-Ireland was the last thing on our minds. We were only three games away, but with the Ulster title at our backs, and with Kildare directly in front of us in the All-Ireland quarter final, Jim McGuinness just wanted us to think of winning one more game. That was for starters, and after that? That was the great unknown.

McGuinness was concentrating on Kieran McGeeney. He had been spouting about how cynical Donegal were, and McGuinness wanted to retaliate, I could see that, but he didn't say anything publicly. In the dressing room, however, he kept talking to us about McGeeney.

Castlefin is a tiny little place between Ballybofey and Lifford. The Finn river flows by the town which is also close to the border with Tyrone. It's a pretty little village in the day time. At night, however, in the middle of winter, nobody would think of taking a spin to Castlefin.

At the start of the year we had nowhere with decent floodlights to train. The Centre of Excellence in Convoy would not open until 2013, so we were happy for the people of Castlefin to take us in. And thankful, even though there can hardly be a field as bleak and entirely barren, and wholly unprotected from the driving rain and winds. We had nowhere else to go.

There were nights we nearly perished to death in Castlefin. No matter how hard the training was, Castlefin could get into your bones. And, on top of that, when Jim and Rory stopped the training to deliberate and reinforce what we were supposed to be doing, and got into their long conversations, there was a danger of a man dying from exposure up there.

It was a narrow wee ground, but it was certainly up on a great height. That meant that the field, even in the depths of winter, had perfect drainage. The dressing rooms were also tight. Each could take 15 men, 20 with a fair push.

Every evening from the beginning of the year, I had taken my seat in the room on the left. I was to be found just inside the door. On the far side of the room, every evening, there was Big Neil, Colm McFadden, Frank McGlynn, Christy Toye and Eamon McGee. Over to my left was Michael Murphy.

Neil McGee, from day one in Castlefin, entered the room on the right. He was in there with Karl Lacey, Anthony Thompson, the Glenties and Ardara connections, the Kilcar boys, and Papa Durcan when he came up from Dublin. Papa preferred the room on the right as well.

In other grounds, on the days of games, in Letterkenny or Ballybofey, Clones, or Croke Park, when we gathered into one big room, seating arrangements went out the window.

We stayed in the Marriott Hotel in Ashbourne, in Meath, the night before we played Kildare. I roomed with Big Neil. It was always him and me together, even though he could snore with the best of them. Paddy McGrath and Neil McGee were always together too. That was another snoring room, but the loudest room of all in Ashbourne, or any hotel in which the Donegal team overnighted, was the room in which Papa could be found. He was the short straw on the team, but Christy Toye was always happy enough to end up in the bed next to Papa.

Christy had no problem sleeping. Christy could sleep in the middle of the road. Laid-back, unstressed, totally relaxed, that was Christy.

Unflappable.

The medical team had arranged for me to visit an ankle specialist. Dr. Alan Lang worked in the Beacon Hospital in Sandyford, in Dublin. The grating feeling and pain that had cut short my Ulster final was still there. He advised me that I would have to undergo an operation to have the small floating piece of bone removed from my ankle joint. An operation would have meant my season was over so we discussed an alternative short term solution and a pain killing injection was decided to be the most effective strategy. The operation would have to wait until the winter months. In the meantime, though, more bloody needles!

It was my job to stop Johnny Doyle.

Doyle was Kildare's greatest servant for over 10 years, and he was also the man who seemed to kick-start McGeeney's boys whenever they needed a boot up the backside in games. Doyle was also a thoroughbred. He was brilliant at picking off his points in the forward line, but Kildare and McGeeney were on their last legs. Or close to it. They had been four years at work together. They were a top eight team in the country all of that time, but it was also time for them to go further.

The pressure was on Kildare.

Doyle, too, was a man who needed to get a greater return after such a long career. He was deserving of more. He was getting on, but he could still run all day long for the good of the Kildare football team. And my job was to stop him in his tracks.

But Doyle was also a hard man to stop. Like Sean Cavanagh, when we played Tyrone in the Ulster championship, it was one of the keys to our gameplan. Doyle took a bang early on when himself and Michael Hegarty raced into one another, and that appeared to underline McGeeney's claims before the game that we were ruthless, and equally cynical, when it came to stopping men.

But Michael Hegarty never took a man out of a game in his life. He was not told to run into Doyle, and it was not something he would even think of doing. On the other hand, I was happy to get in Doyle's way, get in his face. It was my job not to give him a moment's peace.

I had failed to do that to Sean Cavanagh. I knew that McGuinness was not going to give me all day to get to grips with the job that needed to be done on Doyle. I knew that Doyle is also one of those footballers, who from the very start of the game, is going... going... going! Also his football brain was one of the best. On top of all this, being handed man-to-man marking jobs was still something new to me.

I was a footballer, first and foremost. I wanted to be on the ball so with a new focus on my defensive duties, it took a bit of getting used to. But I reckoned I could get the job done. And I also wanted to get down to the other end of the field and hurt them on the scoreboard as well.

Doyle didn't get a score in the game. Or in the extra time that was played. Not a point. I was happy. I also picked off a point myself. He did from time to time go back into the forward lines, and each time I passed him off to one of the boys inside.

Any time he came back into the middle, I had him.

Every time he was on the ball I managed to get a piece of him. He barely had time to breathe. I held him at times. Dunted him when the referee, David Coldrick from Meath, was not looking. There was nothing nasty to it, nothing downright cynical, just a normal day's hard work.

Doyle had featured more than anybody else from Kildare in the DVD clips McGuinness had on hand. I knew that he especially liked to come on the loop, and going at full stride that's how he kicked most of his points.

It was a baking hot June evening in Newbridge when we had last played Kildare in a championship game. It was back in 2001, the year the Qualifiers were first introduced, and a year before I made it onto the Donegal senior panel.

Donegal had lost to Fermanagh in the first round in Ulster after a replay. Fermanagh had become a pain in the arse for Donegal in those early years after the turn of the millennium. They beat us by a point in Brewster Park. Getting a second bite through the Qualifiers was a whole new experience, and a gang of us went down to the game.

It was a weekend of fun and drinking, and we stayed overnight in Dublin after the game. A friend of ours, who was a Garda in Dublin at the time, brought us out of Newbridge. The road to Dublin was thronged, but he threw his siren on and we bombed our way in record time out of town and towards the city.

It had looked like the game was heading for injury time, after 70 minutes of end-to-end stuff. It was 1-16 each, amazing entertainment, open football, man to man at both ends of the field, and the game was way deep into injury time when their corner back, Ken Doyle popped up at the other end to punch the winning point.

Corner backs crossing the halfway line was a rarity in those days. There were so many great Donegal footballers out there on the field, Brendan Devenney, Mark Crossan, McGuinness too. Glen's Noel Hegarty was also one of the team's loyal servants who had endured, same as everyone else, almost 10 long years since the All-Ireland win in 1992.

He had told everyone he was going to retire whenever the championship came to a halt in 2001. In the dressing room, after he had spoken to his players, our manager Mickey Moran paid a special tribute to Hegarty.

Hegarty did not respond.

The story goes that he remained sitting, listening to Moran, and when the room fell silent he raised both of his hands in the air.

Fifteen years he had been on the team.

He said nothing.

Only... 'hal-le-f******-lu-jah!'

Noel Hegarty was released from duty as a Donegal footballer.

Michael Hegarty used to tell the story of Noel's brother, Paddy Hegarty. He was another fine footballer who played with Donegal and Naomh Columba. He was talking about the fitness levels of the Donegal team on one occasion.

Nowadays the same man is a full time coach with the County Board, but when he was younger you would spot Paddy up on the hills around Glencolumbcille tending to his sheep.

'Fit boys, no doubt,' he smiled, looking at the latest brand of a Donegal footballer, but he wasn't totally overawed.

'But in our day,' he continued, 'Ya knew ya were fit... when ya would be carrying the sheep dog home on your back at the end of the day's work!'

There was also a single point between the teams on the second last day of July in 2011. Just under 40,000 people got to witness a game of football that was a million years removed from the gambling nature of the game in Newbridge in 2001.

McGeeney and McGuinness had their cards closer to their chests than perhaps any two managers had ever kept them in Croke Park.

At six o'clock, Michael Murphy had led us on our pre-match parade and anyone looking could see that he was clearly not himself. He was definitely limping. The hamstring was not good. McGuinness knew that the Kildare boys would be having a good look at Murph. And he wanted to keep them thinking right up to the very last seconds.

McGuinness knew that even the slightest distraction could work in our favour. He also knew that it was too risky to start Murph, and it had been decided that David Walsh would replace him once the teams took their positions.

No Michael Murphy on the field when the ball was thrown up was sure to cause some confusion for the Kildare boys, and also for McGeeney and the handymen around him on the sideline.

McGuinness then wanted to keep them guessing.

Would Murph come onto the field at all?

And, if he did, when would he appear?

Nobody likes to be spending their time at guesswork while a match is at full tilt, but after 23 minutes McGuinness sent Murph in for Paddy McBrearty. Murph kicked three points, one from a free kick, in the helter-skelter game which developed through the second half and into extra time.

McGeeney had Kildare primed for a big performance, and they played like a team confident of winning a place in the semi finals. They had us in trouble on the scoreboard early in the second half. They led 0-6 to 0-3. There were 41 minutes gone when their big full-forward Tomas O'Connor was ruled to have been in the square when he claimed a ball that rebounded off the post. Doyle had taken that shot. It looked like his first point of the game, but it came back into play.

O'Connor hammered the ball past Papa.

But Coldrick and his umpires got it wrong and ruled that he had been in the small square when he got possession. It showed on TV afterwards that O'Connor's goal should have stood, and that we should have been 1-6 to 0-3 behind. That moment in the game had, however, told us we were about to go out of the championship.

We responded immediately. Murph, Ryan Bradley and Dermot Molloy hit three quality points. And it was a draw match, 0-7 each, when Christy Toye got his first touch of the ball.

Christy was the fastest man with the ball in his hands on our team. It was impossible for the rest of us to work out exactly how he could solo with the ball at such a pace. At times he was faster soloing the ball than sprinting without it, as crazy as that sounds.

He could just take off.

And nobody would be able to go with him. Christy was one of the three young men who really stood out when we all landed in the Donegal squad at about the same time, 2000, 2001 and 2002. There was him and McFadden from St Michael's, and Gweedore's Kevin Cassidy. They were the three men to watch. I was behind them. I had to wait for my opportunity, but they went straight onto the team. But the previous 25 months had been mostly a wreckage for Christy because of injuries.

As soon as he came in against Kildare, Christy took the ball and calmly slid it past their 'keeper, Shane Dowling. It was his first touch in all those months. After that, the game went off the radar. It was brilliant and it was also bedlam. The rain and the floodlights helped. The game went into orbit.

Neither McGuinness nor McGeeney had prepared for anything like it. Afterwards, when it was all finally over, McGuinness was like a man fuelled by something that is normally reserved for a Maserati or a Formula One car. Like the rest of us, he had never witnessed so much in just one game. There was our courage and sheer guts, for starters, but the individual displays were beyond even our own belief. Neil McGee stood out from everyone else at full back.

But Karl Lacey stood out even further than Neil.

Karlo gave the greatest individual display that anyone in Donegal could ever remember seeing, from any man on any team, in Croke Park.

His covering in defence, and his breakouts were spell-binding. With everyone else struggling to reach three-quarters pace in the dying minutes, Karlo was still surging forward. When the rest of us were out on our feet he was still tackling like it was the first minute of the game.

Of course, Karlo had been blazing a trail long before Jim McGuinness came near us. He was hands down the best corner back in the game. He had his Allstar awards to prove it. He churned out incredible performances from day one, snuffing out every opponent in his path.

He had always trained harder. He never seemed to be out of breath. Karlo played on autopilot. And his hand speed? It was phenomenal. I'd watched him in the gym first thing in the mornings and, pound for pound, there was nobody stronger.

Karlo was also private. One of the quiet ones, usually sitting at the top of the bus while all of us card sharks did our business down the back. He must have been so pissed off with all the drinking and messing up that had been done for so many years, by most of us, but, never, ever, did he say a word to anybody.

The scores were few enough throughout.

We won the long game by 1-12 to 0-14. With 82 minutes gone Emmet Bolton had kicked a killer point to put them three ahead, 0-14 to 1-8. It might have been the dagger to our heart. Getting up to their end of the field was no longer something like a 100 yards run by then, it was more like half a mile.

Murph was a miracle worker, like Neil and Karlo, and popped over a score from a pull-back from Frank McGlynn. Then he floated over one of his mighty frees from way out to reduce the difference to a single point, and when the teams finally drew level it was Murph, still not one hundred per cent fit, who somehow got his hand to the ball as it was about to go over the sideline. His flick up under intense pressure was sheer class. The ball got worked out to Cass and he kicked the winning score.

It was an awesome shot. One of those scores that is usually kicked in the opening minutes of a game when a footballer is full to the gills with adrenalin and totally fearless.

To kick such a score for us at the death of the greatest game any of us had ever played in left us certain that Cass, as we always had suspected, was a rare breed of a man.

That kick sealed a victory that none of us would ever be able to forget, and sent us through to meet Dublin in the All-Ireland semi final.

By the end of the year, Cass was gone.

Jim McGuinness showed Kevin Cassidy the door, and slammed it shut behind him in early November.

Cass was always an animal of a man. Even as a young footballer, he looked like a toughened veteran. He played like one too. He was 30 years of age in 2011 and ready to go on for another 10 years if he was let. None of us doubted Cass. He'd had his troubles with other Donegal managers. He'd been on and off the squad for disciplinary reasons.

But there was not a man who looked ready to bleed for Donegal as heavily as Cass. He was kicked out for contributing to a book called 'This is Our Year' in which he had told stories about the team and our preparation.

He had broken the team's code by doing so.

In the weeks and months after McGuinness told him to go there were stories in the newspapers about Kevin Cassidy, and every last man on the Donegal squad, signing contracts. Some people even spoke about these being legally binding documents governing our behaviour, and our roles within the squad.

But that was just total nonsense.

At the start of 2011, and at the beginning of each new season after that, Jim McGuinness left a blank sheet of paper on a desk at the top of the meeting room. We queued up and wrote our names, in one long list of signatures, on this piece of paper. Though McGuinness did make a big deal out of it.

It was no blank sheet of paper in his eyes.

He told us we were signing something we needed to commit to, and he warned us that no man could break the bond once they had signed.

There was no contract.

The sheet of paper was symbolic.

We all lined up and waited our turn to sign. But he always let us know that we should only sign the sheet of paper if we were willing to go above and beyond for the good of the team, if we were full sure we wanted to dedicate the next year of our lives to reaching the objectives he had set for us.

'Sign it with you blood...!' shouted Damien Diver, standing at the back of the room. 'Sign it boys... with your... BLOOD!'

Diver had joined the management team for the start of the 2014 season and it was his first time watching us sign.

Murph was always the first to sign.

Cass had signed the sheet. And Cass had broken the bond with every one of us by working with a journalist behind our backs. Now that I am retired and no longer in that group of footballers, I can look back objectively and feel some sympathy for the way Cass was treated. But, at the end of 2011, when I heard what he had done, I wanted nothing more to do with him.

One hundred per cent, I was in agreement with McGuinness. When I talked with Murph or Big Neil, I found that they felt the exact same. When any of us discussed Cass we only asked ourselves, how could he have done it?

We were in a bubble.

We were together in that bubble. Nobody had any right to act independently in that bubble. We were all offended.

It was treachery.

If I had met him on the street at that time, I would have crossed to the other side rather than talk to him. My anger was pure.

McGuinness did not warn us that he was going to kick Cass out. We heard it on the grapevine the same as everyone else in Donegal, and McGuinness never talked about it when we were back together preparing for 2012.

At the time I was delighted.

Now, however, I have to admit I'd actually cross the street to talk to Cass if I did see him. I ask myself, now, if Jim McGuinness was right to cut him as he did without hesitation and with absolutely no mercy?

I have softened since the end of 2011. I am no longer one of them, one of the men in the dressing room, and I ask myself also that if I was Donegal manager in 2011 would I have done that to Cass?

Dublin played a zonal back six.

Every time, their defenders passed Donegal men off to one another if there was a switch. In the centre of their defence, Ger Brennan was barking out orders, making sure he had a man either side of him at all times. Dublin were not going to be pulled out of shape. There was so much pressure on Dublin, and also on their manager Pat Gilroy. They had so much to lose. Not just if they lost to us in the All-Ireland semi final. The whole country was on

Dublin's and Gilroy's back, and they were not going to take risks. It was 16 years and counting since they had been in an All-Ireland final.

Deep into the second half when we badly needed to get scores, every time we won the ball back and moved up the field, we were met by this wall of Dublin defenders. However, our biggest problem in the final quarter of the semi final was not that wall especially, it was that we did not support the man on the ball enough.

Too many Donegal footballers were left on mini kamikaze missions every time we launched a raid out of our own defence.

It was a whole different game to the quarter final win over Kildare. This time it was a classic chess match. In the second half we struggled badly to get to the heart of their defence, though it was a different story in the first 35 minutes. And we led by 0-6 to 0-3 midway through the second half. And at the start of the second half, Colm McFadden had broken through and he belted the ball hard and low, but just not low enough to beat Stephen Cluxton in their goal and hit the back of the net.

A goal, then, would have broken Dublin's back.

McFadden hadn't scored against Kildare.

Christy had come in for him and quickly scored his goal, then McFadden had been put back on in extra-time, and then taken off again. It wasn't his worst game, it wasn't his best game. Against Dublin, however, he scored four points, two of them from play, exactly seventy-five per cent of our total. He was immense.

We had always been friends, right back to our school days in St Eunan's. He always got about eighty per cent of our scores, right back to the very first game we ever played together. He single handedly won the MacLarnon Cup for us. He was on the Ireland under-17 International Rules team.

He was a bull of a young man.

We all called him 'The Bull'. He did things his own way.

I don't know who gave him that nickname. I'm guessing it's for one of two things. Firstly, his strength. He had supreme upper body strength. A very difficult man to dispossess when on the ball. And secondly, there was his temper! For a man who messes so much and enjoys the banter, he could lose his cool very quickly if the mood wasn't good!

Football or golf, The Bull could get mad as hell. The last time I played golf with him was in Fanad, on a lovely tranquil afternoon made for 18 holes in Portsalon. We were on the fairway, on a big par five, four of us, myself and Big Neil, Daragh Gallagher (who was on the panel from Naomh Conaill), and Colm.

There was a group ahead of us, holding us up just a little and so we took our time looking for Daragh's ball in the semi-rough. We knew there were a few bucks coming onto the tee box behind us, but we had nowhere to go, we couldn't play our next shots. Eventually, Daragh chipped out.

We were in the middle of the fairway, finally, ready to play our second shots when a ball suddenly whistled over our heads.

*'What the f***?'*

What was that about, we asked ourselves?

'Jesus Christ... that almost split one of us!' said Big Neil.

'What should we do?' I asked.

*'I'll tell you... what I'm going to f****** do!' announced McFadden.*

McFadden was marching over to the ball that might have killed one of us. He picked it up. And he threw the ball hard across the fairway. It disappeared into a mass of bushes. We played on.

We were still laughing on the next tee box, a par three, which headed back towards the previous hole.

'I've seen lads get kicked out of golf clubs for less than that!'

'Picking up a man's ball... throwing it away?'

'They'll never let you in again.'

'You're finished McFadden... banned from Portsalon for life!'

We were all giving it to him as one of the bucks from the previous group was marching towards us.

McFadden, who is a good golfer, was having none of it. 'They didn't even... SHOUT,' he protested, still a little pink in the face with anger. 'NO FORE FROM THEM... NOTHING!'

The buck had bounded up right in front of us.

Big Neil knew him, because Big Neil seems to know everyone. But Big Neil said nothing. Big Neil was just smiling at The Bull.

'Anyone see a Nike 3 golf ball there... boys?' the buck asked.

The Bull stepped forward.

'Aye...' said The Bull, '... I'll tell you exactly where it is...

'... IT'S BACK IN THAT WHIN BUSH...

'BACK THERE!'

McFadden then placed his ball on the tee and took a practice swing.

Michael Darragh Macauley never wanted to be touched any time I played against him.

How dare you touch me!

He did not shout that at me, but I knew he wanted to.

*How dare you f****** touch me!*

That's what he was saying to himself.

*Who the f*** are... YOU... TOUCHING ME?*

Macauley hated being pulled and dunted. And I knew what he wanted to say to me, but instead he would start throwing his elbows back at me. I'd usually take two or three of those shots, but even if I got one on the side of the head I didn't mind. I knew I was really getting to him.

Ryan Bradley and myself were in the middle of the field in the All-Ireland semi final in 2011. Big Neil was out. My job was to take Macauley. Ryan took Denis Bastick. It was not a man marking job this time. It wasn't the same job I had been given in the quarter final on Johnny Doyle.

McGuinness told me to continue working within our defensive system, and to get back all of the time when the ball broke down, to our first line of defence. When Macauley got the ball, then I had to go out and take him. Or when he was running towards our line without the ball, I also had to take him.

He's a big threat when he's coming from deep with the ball, but McGuinness still didn't want me man marking him. He wanted me to wait. And McGuinness knew that Macauley usually received the ball about 50, 60 metres out from the opposing goal, and that I was always going to be back there, close enough to Macauley, the second he got onto it.

My job was then to meet him at the beginning of his powerful runs. If Macauley gets running for 15, 20 yards he is a hard man to stop at that point. I had to get to him earlier than that. My job was to be on him within two or three seconds, less if I could. I had to close down his space. Get in his face. Wear him down. Annoy him. That's what I did in the semi final, and again in the semi final in 2014.

In 2014 I nearly had my shirt torn off me in the first few minutes. He was flailing and pushing, and throwing those elbows. I knew he was highly agitated and the game wasn't even 10 minutes old.

He was staring me down.

I could see, once again, what he was thinking. I felt in 2014 that I knew his game inside out. I also knew that he was not expecting me to play in the semi final in 2014. Next thing, he saw me trotting towards him in the middle of the field.

I grabbed a hold of him.

In the opening minutes I was holding his jersey down hard with both hands as he was trying to get a run for one of Stephen Cluxton's kick outs. The elbows came back at me.

I took one good dunt on the point of the chin.

It didn't matter, I still held him tight. Then he started shouting at me. He called me a f****** tramp.

Good.

The next time I bumped into him, two or three minutes later, I took a tighter hold of his jersey.

We were two points each after nearly half an hour of the 2011 semi final.

We had them completely closed down. We also knew that they had been practicing on the training field ways in which to break us down. Whatever they had been at, they looked wholly unable to tear down any part of our defence. At the other end, McGuinness left Colm McFadden mostly isolated.

Except he was surrounded by a posse of blue jerseys. Any time McFadden actually won the delivery of the ball into him, they swarmed around him. He still managed another point before half-time, just after Kevin Cassidy broke upfield and kicked a second with the outside of his left boot. We led 0-4 to 0-2 at half-time.

Then Colm had that chance to score the goal which might have sent

Dublin into mass panic. The point, nevertheless, increased our lead. Thirteen minutes later we led 0-6 to 0-3, and Dublin were a team still trying to piece clues together as to how they might try to win the game.

We finished with that same number of points.

It was pitifully small.

Too small, we discovered, to be sure of winning a game of such importance. They also finished on a small number. Eight points, with only two of them coming from play. Our plan to stifle them worked just about perfectly. Cluxton ended up their second highest scorer. Only one of their starting forwards grabbed a point from play. And Dublin's first score from play did not come until the 60th minute. Close to perfection, but not quite.

We did not manage another score after the 44th minute.

In the All-Ireland Under-21 final, in 2010, Rory O'Carroll had beaten Murph all day to direct ball that was not played long enough. O'Carroll stood in front of Murph all through that match. That's the way he liked to play.

We knew that if we sent him laterally maybe he would be exploited.

So, how did we not manage to beat Dublin?

We didn't put enough pressure on Ger Brennan, and did not give Murph the chance to make O'Carroll look ordinary. Most of all, we did not have enough men supporting the man racing out of defence with the ball. Karlo had taken a hard knock from Barry Cahill and had to be substituted. We were robbed of that type of player who could get ahead of the ball.

We did not give ourselves the chance to build a score to win the game. Meanwhile, Pat Gilroy brought Kevin McManamon in for Barry Cahill at half-time, and McManamon immediately started to work at prising open our front line of defence with his darting solo runs. Bernard Brogan kicked a free over the bar. Cluxton kicked a 45, and then on the hour mark McManamon got their first score from play. They had also lost Diarmuid Connolly to a red card by then. But they were the only team making scoring chances.

Bryan Cullen grabbed the point that gave them the lead. The ball fizzed across in front of me, and I went to dive for it, to try to block it, but at the last second I stopped. I thought it was going out of play.

I hadn't seen Cullen behind of me.

Cass was furious.

I could not hear what he was shouting in my direction. He was marking Cullen and he was sure I had the ball. He was growling at me. Snarling. He knew the game was up.

I knew it too.

It was defence or bust the whole second half, and we had gone bust when Cullen rifled over that point.

Five minutes later, Bernard Brogan whacked over another free kick. 0-8 to 0-6, and no doubt about it, we had almost hit all of our targets defensively. We had set out to keep them under 10 points. Eight or nine points was actually what we had spoken about. We knew we could keep them down to a score that low.

Jim McGuinness had spent the whole year, and every hour he could get his hands on between the quarter final and the semi final, working on our defence, refining it, reinforcing it.

On the training field, we knew exactly where we had to be every time in defence. There was almost an 'X' on the field for every man to find in defence, and Jim had worked so hard with us it was like he had marked out those 'Xs' with the studs from his own football boots.

We had, I believe, a real fear of moving out of defence and bringing the ball up the field. I knew I had a reluctance to commit myself forward.

We had the perfect defence in our brains.

I did not get into a single scoring position the whole game against Dublin. Not once. I was afraid to give anything away, even an inch of the field to Dublin. It was not like McGuinness had called for one of his famous '6s' and locked us all into defence. He did no such thing.

We all went into 'lockdown' ourselves.

We defaulted to the 'lockdown' when we had built up our lead early in the second half, and that is what lost us the game.

Three hours before the game, back in our hotel in Ashbourne, McGuinness had actually presented us with the team and how he wanted us to play. He wanted to wait until the final minute, if he could. He wanted nothing getting out. He laid out the whole plan.

Who was taking this Dublin player... that Dublin player... the role of every single Donegal player was laid out on paper. Our phones were collected and put away. McGuinness wanted total focus.

'Dublin are going to have to run the ball,' he told us. 'That'll be their only option as their full-forward line will become redundant.

'What are they going to do when they look up and see a Bernard Brogan being marked by Neil McGee from behind... and David Walsh sweeping in front of him?

'They won't be able to kick the ball...

'... so what option do they have left?

'They're going to have to run the ball.

'You might hear boos from the crowd.

'Don't let that deter you... by half-time Dublin might only have a point or two scored. We can hold them to eight... nine points.

'Stick to the plan.

'It's not going to be pretty.'

We had only three hours to understand it all fully and make it work. And we had made it work. We had made an incredible success of McGuinness' gameplan, but we were out of the All-Ireland championship.

We had been honest.

But we had not been courageous enough against Dublin in 2011. In 2012, we assured ourselves that we would be more courageous.

2012

CHAPTER 5

'CAN I TRUST YOU?'

If there were four words Jim McGuinness wanted to have cemented into our heads in 2011 it was those four.

On the training field every second night, in the dressing room before games, and at half-time, he kept asking the same question. 'Can I trust you... can I TRUST you?'

It is not the hardest thing in the world to build energy in a room packed with grown men who are bursting to be successful and win something. But McGuinness knew how to build and control that energy.

He wanted each of us to buy into the question he was asking. It was a question he also wanted us asking one another.

'Can I trust you?'

In 2012, he had a different phrase.

'HOPE YOU MISS!'

That's a 'Hope you miss' attitude, he'd tell us.

That's a 'Hope you miss' tackle, he'd announce, looking at the man who had made a half-hearted attempt to get to his man on the DVD we had been watching.

This phrase did not dominate McGuinness' speeches until late in the summer of 2012, and after we had beaten Kerry in the All-Ireland quarter final. It was Neil McGee who first got it in the ear from McGuinness.

There was a moment in the first half of that game where Colm Cooper, suddenly, momentarily broke away from Neil, who found himself three or four yards away from The Gooch, and all at sea. The Gooch spun and clipped the ball over with his left peg.

Before we played Cork in the semi final, McGuinness zeroed in on that score. And he kept at it, refusing to leave Neil's mental lapse alone. Stopping the DVD and rewinding, stopping... rewinding... unrelenting.

'What is that?' McGuinness asked of us all.

'What is that?' he repeated.

'That is not us.... that is f****** not us!

"You know what that is?

'I'll tell you what that is!

'It's... a... hope you miss attitude!'

One lapse could cost us a game, he stated.

One moment... one man wishing... hoping he misses, and the championship could be over, he insisted.

Two or three yards, he warned us, could make the difference between being All-Ireland champions in 2012 and winning nothing.

McGuinness and all of the boys had holidayed in Florida at the very end of 2011. Kathryn and I were getting married the following week so we didn't make the trip. We honeymooned in South Africa.

Part of me missed not being with the boys, but a larger part of me just wanted a peaceful end of year with Kathryn, to enjoy our private time together, to step away from the pressure of being part of a winning team. I relaxed and chilled, slept well and ate very well. I did a lot of reading. I lounged by the pool.

We got a car and drove down the coast.

Our wedding day and all of the glorious memories of that day mingled with the reflections of Croke Park, and the remorse of losing to Dublin the way we did. Jim had brought us all together not long after losing that game.

It was an evaluation session in which he wanted us all to understand how we had fallen down in the All-Ireland semi final. He also wanted to do some understanding himself so that he could build us into a stronger team in 2012. He knew we had to score more. We were the best defensive team in the country. We had broken all sorts of defensive records in 2011. We took great pride in that but now we needed to score more, another five or six points more in each game at least.

Pat Spillane had called us the Taliban of the football world. Jim McGuinness wanted us to stuff those words, and any other insults, down the throat of Spillane and all of the other boys in the RTE studios.

He wanted us to remember how we had been disrespected through the year, and he wanted us to share his anger.

I think Jim McGuinness was annoyed with himself too at the manner in which 2011 had ended. The way we ran the football against Dublin was not good. At times it was terrible. We were getting isolated, running into tackles, and there was not enough support for the man with the ball. That support had to be there all of the time.

At the meeting that closed down 2011 we had identified those problems, and from the very start of 2012 we began working on solving them. We focused more closely than ever before in training at how we ran the ball out of defence.

We needed a man ahead of the ball carrier, we needed men left and right, we needed a man behind the ball carrier. All of the time. Every single time we won the ball back in our own half of the field. We started to train for the transition from defence to attack.

We trained as we intended to play.

Repetition... repetition... repetition... same as 2011, except in the early weeks and months of 2012 we were all running harder, running smarter. McGuinness wanted us to be the best team in the country at not being turned over. We already knew we were the most economical team in the country. McGuinness kept showing us the statistics to back up what he was telling us.

We had the best free takers in the country, and if we could develop a running game to get us into scoring positions, from the hand or from free kicks, we would be able to push our scoring average up to 17 and 18 points per game. We already knew that we were able to keep other teams to totals of eight and nine points per game.

Winning in 2012 needed to be pure science.

Simple maths.

Though we lost our first game in the new league to Down by a single point, 1-10 to 0-9, and all through the Saturday evening in Newry we could hear James McCartan, their manager, shouting and roaring to keep the ball wide, to stretch our defence.

'Keep it... WIDE,' he told them over and over, '...NO CONTACT!'

Other managers had watched us closely in 2011. We quickly understood that we would have to become a lot more intense at pushing out from our lines in defence, and make contact with the other team.

The next week in training they were back to their old mantra.

'Thump him...

'THUMP HIM WILL YA!'

Every time in training, any man who had the ball had to be hounded down.

'Make contact...!

'Thump him...

' ...make CONTACT!

'THUMP HIM...

'... THUMP HIM!'

Some nights, that is all I heard, and driving home from training the same orders would be whirling around in my brain.

We lost by three points to Laois in our second league game. Our score totalled 12 points, still not enough to win tight games. They won 2-9 to 2-6 in O'Donnell Park.

Losing in Letterkenny always hurt more. It was an especially bad defeat and two goals within sixty seconds, eight minutes from the end of the game, gave a false look to the scoreboard. We were bloody awful.

Michael Murphy returned to the team in March with a goal after 14 seconds against Cork, and was with us when we took the bus down to Tralee and faced a Kerry team that had no Tomas O Se, no Colm Cooper, no James O'Donoghue. We bused it down on the Saturday afternoon, and bused it home on the Sunday evening. It was a horrible journey back up the road. It took forever. We had been hammered by Kerry.

We managed 1-8.

They were well on top in the middle and led by 2-10 to 0-6 just after half-time. It was game over. They took it easier to the end and finished with 2-16, double scores. There's always something specially sickening by losing to double scores. We had started well enough, but then we threw in the towel. The speed of their hand passing surprised us. We were putting up our defensive lines but they cut through us like butter. Their passing was clinical. One-twos, and they were through. It was like some of us were stuck in quick sand.

It was shocking.

We had wanted to go down to them and lay down a marker. We knew they would be one of the teams to beat near the end of the season. We knew full well we would probably have to stop them if we were to lift Sam. Losing was a blow to the solar plexus. Our confidence also took a hit. The bus journey home was so damned quiet.

We had suffered three quick defeats.

We had not scored enough, not even close to the targets we had set ourselves at the beginning of the year.

I was questioning myself on that journey home. I was questioning everyone around me. Trust? Could I trust every man on that bus? Could I trust McGuinness' system?

We had bowed down to Kerry.

That's how Jim McGuinness saw it. He had spent some of the best years of his life in IT Tralee, and he deeply loved the Kerry way, but he took that defeat extra personally.

Trust?

It was a big word for a Donegal footballer to use.

None had existed in all my years on the team. And good managers before Jim McGuinness had trusted us.

Mickey Moran, Brian McEniff, Brian McIver, John Joe Doherty! Each of them had found out, the hardest way possible, that trusting every last man sitting around them in the dressing room was a fool's business.

Moran was a great coach. His assistant, John Morrison was something of a genius. Together they were abstract thinkers about the old game, and they were constantly coming up with new techniques in training, new ideas about how to play the game. They also had a decent team at their fingertips.

I was the new boy, but Damien Diver and John Gildea were there, great ball players. McGuinness was there, still as strong and athletic as hell. Paul McGonigle, Michael Hegarty, and Cass who made his debut in 2002 and had a rawness about him, that shaved head look, tough as nails, mad to win every single ball. Christy Toye was playing regularly in the half forward line. Roper, Devenney, Sweeney up front. It had the makings of some team alright.

We had beaten Cavan in the preliminary round of the championship in 2002. Five points, and then I got my first championship minutes against Down in the first round. I got one touch of the ball. I handpassed it off and galloped up the field. I knew in my heart I was barely ready, but Moran and Morrison wanted to see what I could do. We won 3-12 to 1-6.

It was World Cup year. Ireland were in South Korea and Japan, and Roy Keane was kicking his heels at home in England after telling Mick McCarthy what he could do with himself.

I was sitting on the bench in Clones when we beat Derry by two points in the semi final. That same afternoon Ireland were playing Spain in the last 16 of the World Cup. There was a penalty shoot out.

Morientes had scored for Spain in the game itself. Robbie Keane had equalised from a penalty, and the game had gone into extra-time, and then penalties.

Donegal were beating Derry in front of me, but some boy in the crowd behind me had his radio on and was listening to the soccer game. There were no more than a few hundred people in the ground. Everyone was at home watching the soccer. I had one eye on the game. Both of my ears, however, were locked to the commentary from the

The highest point of every footballer's career is to lift the Sam Maguire Cup. Thanks to Jim McGuinness I take my moment on the Hogan Stand after we had defeated Mayo in 2012 and (below) I share a moment with the man himself after we had captured the Ulster title.

The Oaklands crew (back row) Adrian McClafferty and me, and (front row) David Leonard, Ronan McClafferty, Niall McClafferty and Damien McClafferty. Looks like I was the only one to make an effort with the face paint!

My first day at school and (right) all those years later I graduate from Maynooth with Kathryn by my side.

Kathryn and I on our wedding day with Mum and Dad (top) and with Barry and my sisters Una, Tríona, Alma and Donna.

Celebrating our big day with my best of friends, my St Eunan's teammates (above) and some of the Donegal boys (below). Here I am (right) with my full back up team Barry Kavanagh, Niall McClafferty, Cathal Greene, Damien McClafferty and Conall Dunne.

Leading St Eunan's in the parade before the 2014 county final versus Glenswilly (top) and the boys start a big night of celebrations (middle). I get to celebrate the victory with Kathryn and Zoe.

Celebrating after scoring my first championship goal against Down in 2006.

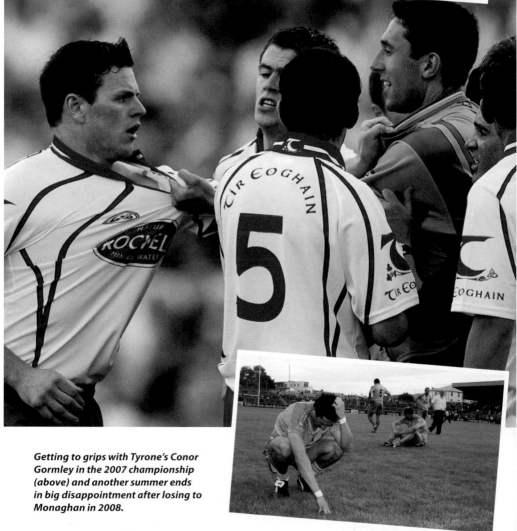

Getting to grips with Tyrone's Conor Gormley in the 2007 championship (above) and another summer ends in big disappointment after losing to Monaghan in 2008.

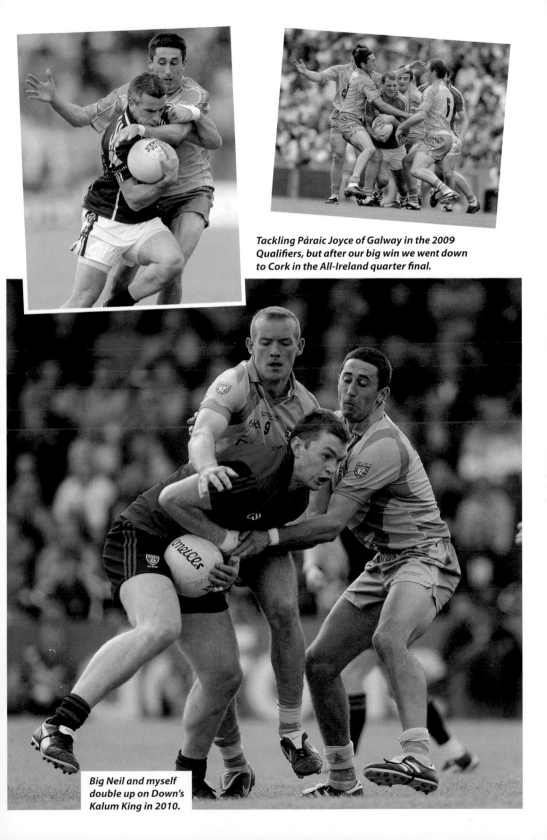

Tackling Páraic Joyce of Galway in the 2009 Qualifiers, but after our big win we went down to Cork in the All-Ireland quarter final.

Big Neil and myself double up on Down's Kalum King in 2010.

Breaking through the Laois defence in the 2011 Division Two league final when victory brought our first title under Jim McGuinness and (below) Title No. 2 was savoured with some passion the minute we got back to our dressing room in Clones after beating Derry in the 2011 Ulster final.

Our All-Ireland quarter final win over Kildare made us believe. I challenge against Robert Kelly (left) and Kevin Cassidy celebrates his match winning point.

Neil McGee refuses to take his eyes off Bernard Brogan in the All-Ireland semi final.

We await the President of Ireland before the 2012 All-Ireland final against Mayo, but never stopped reminding one another what we had to do once the ball was thrown in.

Winning possession in the All-Ireland final.

Kathryn and myself start our night's celebration in the best of company with the Sam Maguire Cup.

The minutes count down as we listen to the National anthem before the 2012 All-Ireland final against Mayo and (below) I get by my old Maynooth teammate, Alan Dillon.

Jim McGuinness, despite the disappointment of losing our Ulster title, stays on the field to honour Monaghan's Ulster final win in 2013 – a tough year for us, though Donegal did have one new supporter as Zoe (top) wears her first county jersey!

Breaking out of defence and away from Alan Freeman during our awful defeat to Mayo in the 2013 All-Ireland quarter final.

I get my marching orders thanks to Monaghan's Darren Hughes in the league final in 2014, however (bottom) on good days and not so good days I always had my best supporters (from left) Una and my brother-in-law Seamus Curran; and at the back Roisin Cannon, my brother Barry, Donna, Kathryn, Alma and Tríona.

We're all ready as we stand together for the National anthem before our victory over Dublin in the 2014 All-Ireland semi final which was perhaps the defining game of the McGuinness era.

I get an earful from McGuinness during our victory over Dublin in the semi final, but it was a game Jim promised us would have goals in it, two of them for Ryan McHugh.

Michael Murphy and myself challenge Anthony Maher and David Moran of Kerry in the 2014 All-Ireland final.

I round David Moran, but defeat in an All-Ireland final is as bitter as victory is sweet.

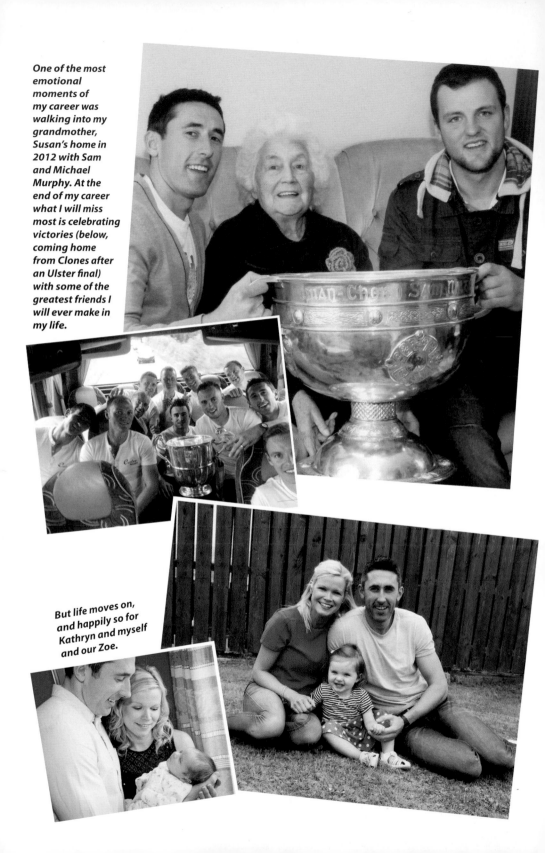

One of the most emotional moments of my career was walking into my grandmother, Susan's home in 2012 with Sam and Michael Murphy. At the end of my career what I will miss most is celebrating victories (below, coming home from Clones after an Ulster final) with some of the greatest friends I will ever make in my life.

But life moves on, and happily so for Kathryn and myself and our Zoe.

radio behind me.

All of us on the bench were living every moment of extra-time, and then the drama of the penalties in the Ireland game.

We were on the edge of our seats.

'Yes!' I shouted as quietly as possible when we scored. We missed three of them and Spain went through to the last eight of the tournament. All of us on the sideline had half-forgotten about the game in front of us. Even though it was still nip and tuck.

That's where our heads were that day.

That's what Mickey Moran had to put up with, and much worse. I don't know if they were aware of what was going on but midway through their final year with us, both Moran and Morrison had their eyes opened. Long before the year was over, in truth, because after we had lost to Armagh by four points in the Ulster final, a few of us took off.

We did a lot of drinking on the Sunday night. The next afternoon a group of us headed over to Glenties. We found McKelvey's pub. I had never been in the place before, but the craic was mighty.

I woke up the next morning, sleeping amongst boxes and wine bottles and stuff on the second floor of the pub. It was the early hours of the morning when we had finished up, and there was no way home. We were an hour from Letterkenny, but the woman who owned the place told us we could spend the night upstairs.

I was on a sofa bed.

Two other boys were on the floor.

The next morning breakfast awaited us downstairs.

We were due to report to training that Tuesday evening. We were still half-drunk. We were talking about the night before, and reminding one another what a great night it had been.

We also talked about the game.

It was mid-morning, that dangerous time after the night before, when things can sour fast. When someone can say the wrong thing?

None of us were that happy.

It was decided we should have another drink or two.

Moran and Morrison had a recovery session prepared for the whole team. There were a few mates and supporters hanging around the pub as well, 10 or 11 of us, and we all left McKelvey's and found another place.

We were in the other pub when Mickey Moran phoned one of us. He rang me. I didn't answer. Then, the phone next to it rang. Nobody answered. One by one. Almost in order around the bar counter. Nobody answered.

We all turned off our phones. Except Brian McLaughlin, who was always one of the nicest boys in the world. A big man, softly spoken.

McLaughlin's phone went again.

He must have felt he was the elder statesman of the group. Some responsibility must have been resting on Big Brian's shoulders, because he answered his f****** phone.

There was silence at first.

'Mickey... Mickey,' replied Brian.

Brian spoke quietly, and with absolute sincerity.

'Mickey... we'll not be there.

'We'll... not make it... sorry Mickey,' he said again with a heavy heart.

'Ah Jaysus... Mickey... we'll not make it!

'We can't make it... Mickey!'

Mickey Moran wanted to know where we were?

'Jaysus, Mickey... we're in a pub.'

More silence.

'We'll not be there, Mickey!'

Someone at the back started singing.

It went 'Olé... Olé, Olé, Olé!'

'Olé...

'Olé...

'Olé... Olé, Olé, Olé!'

McLaughlin hung up his phone, finally, because everyone had burst out laughing. It was lawless stuff.

It was serious shit for any manager to take.

But for good managers to take such behaviour was ten times harder, I can only imagine now. There was a craziness, a madness to our behaviour. A complete breakdown of respect.

Trust?

It went out the window, nearly every year. Often two or three times during the one year. Drinking for two days, sometimes three days after a particular game was something that would happen. I don't know whether it came from a sense of entitlement? Or arrogance of some description? I'm not sure, looking back now, what it was rooted in?

There was always a group of lads who felt they needed a blow out, and that a 'family tradition' you might call, should be maintained.

Of course we were deluded, and selfish.

We all made it home that Tuesday night. And we trooped into training on the Thursday evening.

It was criminal, of course, because in the fourth round of the Qualifiers in 2002 we beat a Meath team that might have won the All-Ireland 12 months earlier. We won 1-13 to 0-14. We wore Ulster's colours. Meath were in Leinster green. Christy was flying. McGuinness was very good. I was happy to be sitting on the bench looking on. Cass was having a great year and would win himself an Allstar award. McFadden was getting lots of game time. Devenney and Sweeney were leading the way up front. Roper and Hegarty were in great form. Gildea, Shane Carr, Barry Monaghan, Noel McGinley... they were bang on, but Christy was leading the way for everyone and he scorched Paddy Reynolds every time he got the ball into his hands.

And we found ourselves in a quarter final with Dublin. We went toe-to-toe with The Dubs, 2-8 to 0-14. A replay was due.

But, first, it was time to party again.

We had been staying in the Camden Court Hotel for the first two games, against Meath and Dublin. It was one of Brian McEniff's places, but it was a wrong choice. It was smack bang in the middle of town. There were supporters in and out of the lobby. Nobody could get a minute's peace. Some of the boys went down to the pub at ten and eleven o'clock to meet their friends the night before each game. They were not drinking each of those nights, they were just popping into the Bleeding Horse, to say hello.

It was, still, so wrong, It was cringeworthy preparation for a team with designs on the All-Ireland title. After drawing with Dublin everyone was supposed to travel home on the team bus, but it did not work out like that. There was a fortnight to the replay, and that was more than enough time to party for some of the boys. On the bus, Mickey Moran did a head count.

It did not take long.

There were only a handful of us on board.

Everyone else had their own plans. And the night had started in the players' lounge in Croke Park, where we all ordered our pints after the game.

We were Donegal.

That was how we operated. There was a tradition to upkeep, and perhaps even improve upon by drinking through the summer and winning the All-Ireland.

When we lost the replay, and badly at that, 1-14 to 0-7, there were rows and inquests into the team's behaviour. Of course there were. That was also normal behaviour amongst the people of Donegal.

Have a good look at ourselves, after the event!

Doing so before was not something that dawned on too many people, not until Jim McGuinness landed in amongst us.

Nobody wanted the job of managing Donegal, when Mickey Moran and John Morrison left. It was officially a poisoned chalice. Who on earth would want to come in and give up their precious time to try to guide a bunch of lunatics to become the greatest team in the country?

Brian McEniff was County Board chairman. He was the last man who really wanted the job, but he had a hard time finding anybody else to take it. Brian knew the story. He wasn't a drinking man himself at all. He was a lifetime Pioneer.

But, after Christmas in 2002, Brian McEniff was named as Donegal manager.

I was soloing up the field with the ball.

We were on the break out of defence in Ballyshannon. Mayo had come to town and had laid down a marker from the very first minute. They were 1-3 to 0-1 up at the end of the first quarter, and we had everything to do.

Marty Duffy from Sligo was in charge, and it always seemed to me that Marty was not a fully paid up member of the Rory Kavanagh fan club. He was one referee I could never see eye to eye with, and shortly before half time, as I was making my break, Kevin McLoughlin grabbed me by the arm. He was pulling and dragging me back.

I threw my elbow back to free myself. I caught him on the head, but he still went down easy enough.

Marty Duffy gave me a straight red.

It was harsh. But I had to take my medicine, which meant I missed out on an amazing fightback, led by Murph who kicked three excellent points from play in a personal total of five points. I also looked likely to miss playing Dublin six days later in Croke Park.

Taking on The Dubs under lights in Croke Park on a Saturday evening is one of the highlights of the early season for every player all over the country. We decided to appeal the decision, which meant I would be in Croke Park 24 hours before the rest of the boys, attending a disciplinary hearing on the Friday evening.

While Murph finished Mayo off and did most of the damage in our 0-17 to 1-7 win, he was not alone in finally kick-starting our year. McFadden and Big Neil got through a tonne of work, and Karlo and Leo McLoone punched countless holes in the Mayo defensive lines. We had now beaten Cork and Mayo in the league, and were no longer staring relegation in the face, though it was still a worry, and we needed a good result against Dublin to free ourselves from that possibility.

I arrived into Croke Park at 9.0 pm on the Friday evening. And I didn't get back to our team hotel in Ashbourne until 3.30 am.

Over six hours.

That's how long I had been on one of the top floors in the ground awaiting my fate. I was so pissed off.

Ciaran McKeever was one of those boys up before me having been sent off against Laois.

I was waiting in a room next door to the hearing with Maxi Curran and our liaison officer Michael McMenamin. McGuinness wasn't about. I was fed up waiting. I was starving, and I was so annoyed that even if I was given the green light to play against Dublin, I told Maxi I'd struggle to get my head around the game.

Someone came in to us with sandwiches and tea some time around midnight. The Armagh hearing had gone on for half the night. They did everything but call in Amnesty International for back up.

My appeal was based on the video evidence from the game

I was also told not to say very much once I got in there. I was warned to choose my words carefully, and not sound aggressive in my self-defence, and not even use any words that hinted at aggression.

If I crossed that line, my goose would be cooked by the dozen or so elderly gentlemen on the committee. They were all waiting for me, sitting around a big Board Room table. I looked at my watch, it was approaching 2.0 am.

F**** this, I thought.

All advice was half forgotten by the time I entered the room. They had our game against Mayo waiting for me on a big screen and they asked me to talk them through the incident.

Easy Rory, I told myself.

Calm as a breeze... do as you were told!

What I really wanted to do was to stand up and tell the whole crowd of them that their hearing, and the whole damned night, was a shambles.

But you're not going to say that!

Be nice... just be happy and sound completely innocent.

I began to talk my way through the DVD clip, and quietly explained that I had just been trying to free myself from my opponent's grasp.

I then said that I had made minimal contact with him.

They was the wrong two words.

F*** it.

Minimal!

And Contact!

I was nailed straight away, by my own mouth. By my admission that I had actually hit McLoughlin.

I left the committee room.

Fifteen minutes later I was called back in. They must have been tired after their whole night's talking. My appeal was unsuccessful.

I didn't get to play against Dublin the next night.

I didn't get to do some more work on Macauley, who had a big performance for them. We played well. We fought back in the third quarter. It was 0-11 each at one stage. Then we lost Murph, and then we lost our concentration as well and they scored two late goals in injury time from Bryan Cullen and Diarmuid Connolly. The performance was not nearly as bad as the 2-16 to 0-13 final scoreline looked.

It was down to the final league game of the season, against Armagh, to decide who joined Laois in Division Two.

I decided to let off a bit of steam by heading out in Dublin with two of my good mates from home Cathal Greene and David O'Herlihy. It was a Saturday night game and I could arrange to get a lift home the following day. I wanted to put the whole weekend behind.

'Meet you both in the Big Tree in 20 minutes,' I texted them.

I didn't wait for the final whistle.

I had seen enough. I grabbed my bag in the dressing room and was gone in a taxi in less than five minutes.

Every night in training, McGuinness was demanding more and more from us. We were all worried about the poor start to the season, but there was no backing off. Jim and Rory drove us harder than they ever had in Castlefin.

Any panic, or creeping doubts, were soon skedaddling out of sight once we arrived in Castlefin.

And between the league and the championship, he further raised the stakes on the training field. Our training sessions were not the normal 60 minutes, or 90 minutes on a big night.

Some of our sessions were two and a half hours long.

We worked on our patterns.

Then we got into the huddle and listened to McGuinness and Gallagher, and then we went back to work. He wanted everyone to know their role down to a tee. In games he did not want us to have to think about what needed to be done.

Every week we had hours and hours of repetition. McGuinness did not want us to believe in a system anymore.

He wanted us to become the system.

Drills were repeated, and repeated, all night long if necessary. If something broke down, we started again. McGuinness, like he did in 2011, was again marking imaginary lines on the field with his football boot. But they were more than imaginary. The 20 points on the evaluation form had changed from 2011 to 2012. It was added to, tweaked. It was refined, based on our feedback from the previous year. When we were on the training field those points were coached every single night, until they became crystal clear in our heads. We then coached each other when we fully understood what he was asking from us.

We were the system.

There was no system if we were not where we were supposed to be when our opponents had the ball. My job was always to get to the arc of the large square. Nothing should distract me. In 2011, I might have thought of tackling a man as I tracked back to defence, but in 2012, even if an opponent was soloing the ball right next to me and I had half a chance of dispossessing him, I knew better to ignore him and get back to my X in defence.

In training, if we were not getting our defensive shape within four or five seconds, McGuinness would go slightly berserk. He would lose the plot completely.

He wanted everyone in place that quickly.

Did we sprint to get there every time? We had to ask ourselves.

If someone failed the system, he'd blow it up and interrupt the training game. He's call for punishment, not just for the man who had failed the system, but for everyone. Press ups all round.

We would start our press ups.

He'd be standing over us.

Shouting down at us.

'Our defensive shape is our... platform to attack!'

Over and over, he'd shout.

'Our... DEFENSIVE SHAPE..

'... IT'S OUR PLATFORM... TO ATTACK!

'DO YOU HEAR ME... BOYS?

'OUR PLATFORM TO ATTACK IS OUR... DEFENSIVE SHAPE!'

But, at home, as I awaited the summer and the championship, like every other player I was still wondering if 2011 was just one of those memorable years, that had always come, and were gone again much too quickly, in the history of the Donegal football team.

I wanted more.

We needed a sign.

A game which would launch us into 2012, and leave us in no doubt that we would go as far again in the championship as 2011.

Further?

That game was a long time coming, but on April 8, in Ballybofey, we were left convinced that 2012 could deliver us anything we wished. It was a huge performance against Armagh.

The victory was like a dam bursting.

We had to play without Murph, and we also lost Neil McGee. There was no Christy either. But the three men came out onto the field after the game and joined our huddle. We were still in Division One. Armagh were gone down. We huddled tightly for the first time all year and told ourselves that nothing was going to stop us.

When the huddle broke and we walked off the field there was a rousing reception from the supporters who had made sure to stick around. The hairs lifted on the back of my neck. Our people wanted to tell us that they were still with us, that they believed in us, and had never doubted us for a second.

We had indeed shown some resolve to beat Armagh. Like every game in the league in 2012 it was a struggle. Michael Stevenson gave an exhibition of free taking for them, and hardly missed a thing, finishing with seven points. They were 0-7 to 0-5 up at the break.

McGuinness laid into us in our dressing room with questions he wanted answered in the second half. But Stevenson stretched that lead to four points within five minutes of the restart.

We worked our socks off to get level.

Marty O'Reilly kicked the equaliser, but then Jamie Clarke won the ball and with some of his magical footwork sidestepped Papa. The ball struck the upright. It was the first lucky break we had received in months.

I kicked the point that put us in front for the first time the whole afternoon. I managed three points.

And we won by three.

CHAPTER 6

Michael Murphy was not the boy wonder in Donegal for very long. He was MAGIC MIKE!

That's what myself and my mates began to call him as soon as he landed on the senior team, and quickly enough he was our official leader. Our captain.

The dynamic in our dressing room changed.

Before McGuinness, I counted myself amongst a bunch of senior footballers who felt entitled to have their say, and to help others. There was Karlo and the McGees, Barry Monaghan, Cass, and Big Neil in his usual quiet and understated manner.

All of us, barking out orders about defence. Reminding one another about how we were going to play the ball into attack. All of this last minute stuff had been part and parcel of our dressing room, and then the manager would quieten everyone and have his specially chosen words.

All that was stopped.

Even in the dressing room at training sessions, or out on the training field, McGuinness would not tolerate listening to a player being 'f***** out of it' by one of his teammates. It was a question of respect.

McGuinness wanted to be the single voice at work at all times. He wanted to protect his players and, at the same time, conserve our energy.

He would raise his voice, but only when he was issuing a specific instruction to us as a group, or whenever he wanted to one hundred per cent get though to one individual.

He was calculated.

When he was finished, he would turn it over to Rory to say a few words. And then both of them would leave it to Murph.

Murph was only 21 years old at the beginning.

It might have appeared absolute madness asking him to take all of that pressure and responsibility, on top of his own thoughts about the game that lay ahead.

But McGuinness had worked with him at Under-21 level. He knew he was level headed, that he had a particular mindset. That he was a born leader.

I knew all of that to be true.

Murph and I were good mates, and we would talk a lot about the game. We would go for lunch and we would play a lot of golf too. I was closer to Big Neil, and Murph and Big Neil were clubmates, so I also became tighter with Murph than most of the boys.

When Murphy spoke in the dressing room, he did not go in for barking and roaring. He would make wee points here and there, and then as we were about to head out, he would become more assertive, more forceful.

Michael Murphy was still in the early stages of recovery from minor knee surgery when the time came to meet Cavan in the preliminary round of the Ulster championship. We had put up a score of 2-14 against them in the championship in 2011. They scored 1-8.

In 2012, we scored a point less, they scored two points more. We went through to the first round on a 1-16 to 1-10 scoreline. It did not look any more comprehensive than 12 months earlier, but there was a difference. We were thinking of wining the All-Ireland when we gathered in the Slieve Russell Hotel in Cavan the evening before the game.

We were also thinking Cavan, of course.

Our concentration was one hundred per cent, because we were going into the game without Murph!

I was team captain. And I was making my 100th appearance for Donegal.

At our team meeting the night before the game McGuinness demanded to know if we all believed if we could go to the next level, and win the All-Ireland title in 2012?

It was a huge meeting.

McGuinness wanted everyone locked into our target for the year. Murph delivered an inspiring speech. There are times when words can fill you with energy. Charge you with emotion. Make you feel invincible.

'Everyone needs to buy into this...NOW!'

That is what he asked.

'Everyone... everyone of you...

'Are you ready to buy into this...

'... Now?'

It was perfect silence in the background as he questioned us. If a pin dropped, we would all have been startled.

He also asked for total honesty, total belief.

When any one of us spoke up, we felt that we had our hand on a Bible and that we were saying something that was on record. There were no idle words that whole evening.

Some months later, in the Burlington Hotel in Dublin, the night we had won the 2012 All-Ireland title, I was chatting to Martin McElhinney, who called me over to him. He took out his wallet, and inside he had this wee piece of paper. He unfolded it and handed it to me.

Martin had written some things down.

We will win Ulster this year. We will win the All-Ireland!

'When did you write that?' I asked him.

'After that meeting in the Slieve Russell the night before we played Cavan,' he replied.

Cavan had done their homework.

But homework did not compare to the year and a half of work we had been doing on the training field, and even though Cavan started out with a packed defence, and two men up front, and even though they went into an early 0-3 to 0-1 lead, we knew they were amateurs at this new piece of work.

After the game, I was presented with a nice piece of crystal to mark the milestone of my 100th game for Donegal. It was a good moment. But I was more concerned about stepping into Murph's boots and leading the way. Cavan had enjoyed some success at Under-21 level and they had boys with fair sized reputations coming through. I wanted our boys to have real energy when it really mattered in the game.

I also wanted to lead from the front. And with Big Neil for company, that's how it worked out. We dominated when it mattered. I scored three points from play. When Paddy McBrearty was fouled and McFadden blasted a penalty to the net, we were 1-7 to 0-4 in front, and that was the end of that for the afternoon.

I struggled to build a relationship with Brian McEniff.

He is an outstanding figure in the story of Donegal GAA, but he was old style as far as I was concerned. Besides, he was not giving me my game often enough. I was based down in Maynooth College when McEniff got the job at the start of 2003, and he would ring me late at night and ask questions which, at the time, I thought were a little crazy.

'What are you eating?' he'd ask.

'Are you eating too many takeaways?'

'No... Brian,' I'd reply, 'I'm not... I'm eating well.'

Like every other student, I probably had a pizza, or a burger and chips, an hour before he phoned me. He'd then ask me how many press-ups I was doing every night? And how many sit-ups?

I'd tell him 200, or 400, any number that came to mind.

I did not know what to tell him.

I'd make up a number. But he'd say that even an old man like him could do 500, perhaps even 1,000 press ups, same number of sit-ups.

At the same time, I was going out to training twice a week with Tosh McGlynn, who trained the Donegal based players in Dublin. But, back in college, I was living the life. I did train hard for the college Sigerson Cup team, and I had an affinity for the

Maynooth team which contained so many great footballers from all over the country, but, after that, I was going through the motions.

Maynooth had been the third pick on my CAO and I did not know anyone down there, but once I settled in, football had me in its grasp. We had an amazing team. Johnny Kane from Westmeath was there, and he'd win an Allstar in Paidi O Se's first year with them. Dermot Geraghty and Alan Moran had played in an All-Ireland final under John Maughan. Marc O Se and Alan Brogan were there. And Bernard Brogan Senior came and did a few training sessions with us, while Bernard Brogan Junior was in his first year in Maynooth as I was leaving. Other Dubs there included Barry Cahill and Declan Lally, and we had Colm Parkinson from Laois, and Alan Dillon from Mayo. It was a wild panel of footballers.

Ross Munnelly from Laois was also with us, and Vinny Corey from Monaghan, whom I shared a house with one year. One morning I woke up and walked out of my bedroom and saw a big, 12 foot sign for The Roost Pub sitting across the top of Vinny's bedroom.

We did not win as much as we should have. Instead, Christy Toye, the McGees, Cass, Karlo, Papa and Dunnion, all of them in IT Sligo were winning Sigerson Cups for fun.

In 2003, I decided to spend the summer in Boston.

I was finished college for the year, and I was sitting on a John McGinley bus on Parnell Square when I worked up the courage to phone Brian McEniff and tell him of my plans. I was going to play for Donegal for the whole summer, but it was the Donegal club team in Boston.

He asked me to reconsider, and told me I was in his plans. But I was barely listening, to be honest.

Brian Roper, Michael Hegarty, Paul McGonigle and Christy were between me and one of the wing forward roles on Brian McEniff's Donegal in 2003. It's only when you're so far away from home you realise the scope the GAA has; real good people like Paddy McDevitt, John McDevitt, Ricky Rushe and Eamon Kelly put their lives into promoting the games on foreign shores. In 2003, however, we lost a replayed final against Cork.

Little did I know that Kathryn, Zoe and I would be back in Canton for the summer of 2015 when we won the Boston title. We went one better to overcome Wolfe Tones by a single point in extra-time with Nicky Kelly from Westmeath and Leitrim's Emlyn

Mulligan getting us over the line. There was such raw emotion from those involved with the club. I hadn't expected that at all. It was great to see what something like that means to the people in a GAA club thousands of miles from home.

Back in 2003, I did not feel any great degree of loyalty to Donegal, and I definitely did not think that I was letting anybody down.

I shared a house with Paidi Swinburn, a college mate, and Dessie Dolan from Westmeath and his girlfriend joined us later. The three months flew by. I was painting and labouring for a living, working with two guys from Kerry and Derry, who were officially lunatics. One of them spent our journey to work skinning up his joint every morning. He'd offer a puff. I'd politely refuse.

'No worries mucker,' he'd shout back to me.

'...steadies me up in the mornings!'

The Tara Bar was our local, and sponsored our football team out there. Donegal had lost in the first round of the Ulster championship before I left home. It was a disastrous four points defeat, 0-10 to 0-6, though nobody could have guessed that the same Fermanagh team under Charlie Mulgrew would battle the whole way to the All-Ireland semi final 12 months later and would be desperately unlucky not to make it to the final itself.

After that, Donegal were presented with an easy trek though the Qualifiers in 2003. They beat Longford by six points and Sligo by five. They beat Tipperary 2-19 to 0-15, and in the fourth round of the Qualifiers put up a strong performance in beating Down 3-15 to 2-10. In the All-Ireland quarter finals they drew with Galway and then beat them by three points within a single week.

On August 31, as I was preparing to come home from Boston, Donegal played Armagh in the All-Ireland semi final. I had watched most of the games, and once Donegal landed in Croke Park I had begun to question the wisdom of my decision to spend the summer abroad.

I wanted them to win, and at the same time I was consumed by selfish thoughts. Donegal lost the semi final, 2-10 to 1-9 to the defending All-Ireland champions. The match swivelled on two incidents, the sending off of our full back Raymond Sweeney, and a classic piece of finishing from Stevie McDonnell which resulted in a heart-breaking goal. Even I felt the pain, so far removed from home.

Brian McEniff intimated after the game that he was going to step down, but he didn't, and I had to pick up the pieces of my Donegal career with Brian still in charge.

'So rock me mama like a wagon wheel
Rock me mama anyway you feel
Hey mama rock me
Rock me mama like the wind and the rain
Rock me mama like a south bound train
Hey mama rock me'

– Wagon Wheel

Old Crow Medicine Show had the song of 2012.

'Wagon Wheel' was written by OCMS's front man Ketch Secor. He mixed it with an old Bob Dylan chorus and the band, who started up by busking in New York State, had a big hit with their folksy bluegrass sound.

After every victory, on the journey home to Donegal, I've lost count of the number of times we listened to 'Wagon Wheel'.

The journey to become the first Donegal team to ever win back-to-back Ulster titles had started out in Breffni Park in Cavan Town. We then had Derry at home in Ballybofey. After that, we were on the familiar road to Clones, where we played Tyrone and Down.

Ulster titles were like pieces of gold to Jim McGuinness.

And they needed to be celebrated seriously.

He had no hesitation in making that decision. The homecoming to Donegal Town as 2012 Ulster champions was as emotional and overpowering as it had been in 2011. The supporters awaiting us looked even bigger in number.

But, first we had taken our time leaving Clones.

As usual, after showering and dressing, we crossed the field to the old minor dressing rooms on the far side of the ground to have our post-match meal. Up the staircase and into the old rooms where we had our own caterers. Nothing too fancy. Chicken curry, followed by trifle and cream, and even though none of us were ever too hungry that soon after a game, we all knew we needed to feed ourselves and be prepared for the long night ahead.

We were all wearing our official team gear. Evolve, a store in Letterkenny, were our clothing sponsors, and they were always generous to us, so it was important to do them proud and take an official team photograph with the Anglo Celt Cup out in the middle of the field.

Same as 2011, there was nobody about.

Just us, and the cup, with pieces of torn paper floating around the empty ground. But it was so special, and personal. All of the pressure, mounting up for days, and getting heavier and heavier in the hours before the throw up, had disappeared. Gone up in a puff of smoke.

The journey home, to Pettigo first of all, always lovely little Pettigo where the locals had a stage constructed next to a wee bar, took just about two hours.

The two nights ahead were all ours.

McGuinness had no trouble allowing us that. On Monday we hooked up in the Reveller Bar in Donegal Town, next door to the Abbey Hotel. We also ended up in other bars dotted around the town. We all bedded down in the Abbey Hotel as well, getting in around three or four o'clock in the morning. The next morning, after a late breakfast, we all got mini-buses back to our own corners of the county.

In every bar during those two nights of celebration, every juke box seemed to be belting out... 'Rock me mama...' every few minutes.

Making history was something profound.

It was not just that we were breaking new ground as a team. Equally important, if not more so, was the fact that we were putting our misguided past, and all of its ridiculousness and craziness, far behind us. Winning back to back Ulster titles was truly going to be something historic.

The win over Derry was an easier battle than we had imagined. Leo McLoone's goal in the 31st minute left us 1-6 to 0-4 up at half-time and that daylight between the two teams was all that we needed. I missed out on the game after once more tearing ligaments in my troubled left ankle in an All

County league clash with Ardara. Ryan and Big Neil lorded it in the second-half and, watching them, I knew I would have to hit the ground running in training if I was to immediately reclaim my starting place in the middle of the field.

It was amazing to sit there and watch the boys in action, to see everything we had spent months working on in training simply come alive in a championship game. I found it mesmerising. Right in front of my eyes, it was happening, just as we had talked and planned it out all those nights in Castlefin.

I watched us turnover Derry's attack, and watched our boys taking off, Ryan and Frank McGlynn and Mark McHugh. In a line, they bombed forward. The passing was inch perfect, the support exactly where McGuinness had told us it needed to be, left and right, in front, behind.

It took my breath away.

We also posted a total of 19 points against Derry in the quarter final - the same as we had totalled against Cavan when we scored 1-16 - and we went better than that against Down in the final when we hit 2-18.

They were the types of scores McGuinness wanted us reaching for, and the only disappointment I guess through the whole Ulster championship was the tightness of our win over Tyrone.

Twelve points was as good as we could manage as Mickey Harte tried to play McGuinness at his own game. It was the ultimate compliment coming from a man who had three All-Ireland titles under his belt, and it caused us considerable difficulties.

We played Tyrone on a Saturday evening.

I had No.19 on my back, but got my game as Rory Gallagher had promised me I would in private phone calls. He told me I'd be starting in the middle. Rory promised me that McGuinness' cardinal rule of only playing men who had been able to train for two weeks would be left to one side on this occasion. I was relieved, but the pressure was on.

Right from the start, from the third minute, after we watched Neil McGee leave the field after pulling his hamstring, the pressure was huge. I was marking Colm Cavanagh. McGuinness wanted a job done on him. Cavanagh had to be worked on.

I continued to distract him, and then I really got into my stride and turned the tables on him. I kicked two points, one after the other, and then McFadden, who had won an amount of difficult ball, took the point of the day. We were 0-12 to 0-8 in front with five minutes remaining.

However, we then dropped back.

In your head you know it is the wrong thing to do, that it is dangerous allowing a team as good as Tyrone to have the ball for the last five minutes and throw everything they have at you. But, we all dropped off all the same, and waited for the final whistle.

With hardly any time left, they clawed our lead back. And there were just three points in it when Martin Penrose skipped his way through a group of us in defence, and got in a low, hard shot.

Papa spread himself and got his foot to the ball.

Papa saved us.

With the likes of Neil Gallagher and Eamon McGee, you always needed to be on your toes, especially when we were away from home. It was like a bunch of kids going on a school tour to Dublin Zoo. Everyone was a wee bit giddy.

At one training camp in 2014, in Albufeira, Colm McFadden and I went back to our chalet after lunch one afternoon. We sat down for a cup of tea with Big Neil and Eamon, who had arrived back before us and put the kettle on.

There was a packet of Oreo biscuits lying open on the table in front of us. Colm and I grabbed one each.

I've a habit of twisting each side of the biscuit before separating it and licking the creamy bit in the centre. McFadden wasn't so strategic. He just bulled in and started munching away.

Eamon and Big Neil sat in silence, still watching the box.

'Are those biscuits a wee bit soggy?' McFadden asked, still chewing.

'Mine is a wee bit minty,' I replied, still licking.

I started to examine my biscuit.

'Mmmmm … minty,' Neil said.

McGee burst out laughing.

'You pricks,' McFadden said. 'What did youse do?'

Colm and I both came to our senses around the same time.

The other two had stuffed the biscuits with toothpaste.

'Mmmmm … minty,' Neil said again.

For the rest of the week at training, Colm and I were called 'Colgate' and 'Aquafresh'.

Big Neil missed the Ulster final because of an ankle injury. Myself and Ryan Bradley started and it was one day, a rare occasion, when Donegal did not miss Gallagher.

The Ulster final, however, was Frank McGlynn's day more than anybody else's. It was one unbelievable goal of his, I have to admit.

That same day in Clones, I was shite.

I think it was definitely one of the poorest games I ever played in my 12 years on the team. James McCartan decided to have me man marked. I had become the specialist man marker on our team, and it was the last thing I was expecting. I had designs on stopping Ambrose Rodgers who had the ability to really lift Down if he started making big catches and got into his stride. My job was to shut down Rodgers.

But I quickly found one of their wing backs, Aidan Brannigan chasing me. He was with me all of the time.

We exchanged a few blows early on. And on one occasion I managed to slip free and I found Deccie Walsh and he put it over the bar.

I thought that would be the end of Brannigan.

Next play, he was back next to me.

Tighter than before, and getting in my way.

Rodgers had bolted through our defence early on and punched the ball over the bar. He could have got a goal. I was nowhere near him. Brannigan had stepped across me, checked my run, and left me dead in my tracks.

*F****** hell.*

I'm going to sort this boy out, I told myself.

I never did. It was so hard to get onto the ball with this boy holding me, and when I went to link up between defence and attack, he managed to check me, every time.

He took his dunts back.

He took them just like I knew how to take them when I was man marking other men. He said nothing.

The more I dunted him and threw my elbow back at him, the tighter he marked me. He knew he was getting to me. And I had to hand it to him, he did an expert job on me.

At the final whistle, Rory Gallagher grabbed me by both shoulders, and asked me was I alright?

'You weren't expecting that!' he told me.

I shook my head.

I didn't want to talk.

I felt devastated with my performance. All around me, boys were shouting and celebrating wildly, but I felt like leaving the field. I was so angry with myself. I also felt sick in my stomach at letting everyone down.

Brannigan and everyone on the Down team felt just as disconsolate at the end. They had not won an Ulster title in 18 years and despite putting up a decent fight in the first half when they levelled it three times, they were soon left for dead and looked as far away as ever from stopping that losing run. Apart from me, we had delivered the perfect performance, and our timing was immaculate, hitting them hard on the scoreboard in the third quarter.

James McCartan, before referee Joe McQuillan even blew his final whistle, had congratulated McGuinness. He saw us simply run away with the game.

Once Murph freed himself from Dan Gordon's shackles, and once they failed to take a couple of goal chances in that first half, they were always heading for trouble and the Down manager knew that.

Ryan Bradley set up Leo McLoone for our first goal just before half-time, and we were only a single point up at the break. But, after that, McGuinness watched us put the burners on.

Kevin McKernan was turned over in classic style, and Murph kicked a score that rattled them. McHugh was dazzling. He kicked a smart point, after taking a pass from Frank.

Frank, for some reason after that score, decided to stay up front. And from the resulting kick out, Murph found him inside. Frank steamed through and scored a goal that any forward would have loved to have finished off.

That left it 2-10 to 0-10. McFadden was on fire. He was getting perfect deliveries from Ryan and Martin McElhinney when he came on.

It finished 2-18 to 0-13.

Two Ulster titles.

Back to back.

History made.

'Rock me mama...'

CHAPTER 7

We were cheering on Kerry.

All around me, as I sat in the Johnstown House Hotel in Meath, our boys were willing Kerry to defeat Mayo in the 2014 All-Ireland semi final.

What's happening here? I thought to myself.

Nobody should ever be cheering on Kerry.

Kerry don't need anyone's support!

We were resting after our morning workout. The next day we were meeting Dublin in our semi final. We knew we had a lot on our plate against Dublin, but McGuinness had told us how we were going to beat them. We had no doubts about that.

Neither, however, did we seem to have any worries about possibly meeting Kerry in the All-Ireland final.

That's what McGuinness had been telling us. He assured us that if we beat Dublin, and did what he asked us to do, then we would also beat Kerry in the final. McGuinness had always warned us never to fear finals.

'Finals take care of themselves...!

'We beat Dublin... then we will not be beaten in the next game...

'Boys, finals take care of themselves.'

I don't like this, I kept thinking.

Cheering on Kerry?

Two years earlier, when we met Kerry in the All-Ireland quarter final, I was told to pick up Tomas O Se.

McGuinness told me O Se's legs were gone.

However, Jim also told me not to let O Se up the field.

'Make it an athletic challenge... you against him Rory!

'Drive at him.

'You'll win frees... he'll not be able to stop you if you run at him!'

I started the quarter final on the wing, and ended up in the middle of the field. But I actually did not have to mark O Se all that closely during the game. Everytime they won the ball, we were racing back into defence.

All of us.

I could see O Se coming up the sideline and not knowing whether to let the ball off to Kieran Donaghy, or whether to have a crack at it himself. Early in the game, Kerry had started shooting from crazy distances. There were balls going wide from all angles.

That's what it is like for teams, even a mighty team like Kerry, when they come up against our system. Our system allows us to play the game on our terms. Every time, we set up our defensive system. And then we tell the other team to come at us and try to break us down?

Kerry were not prepared for that in 2012.

They had no real idea what to do with the ball.

While McGuinness had ordered me to make it an athletic challenge against O Se, that was easier said than done. It was fine when I had the ball. I was able to run directly at him, and be really aggressive in taking him on. It was more difficult when he had the ball.

Tomas O Se is one of the greatest footballers of the last 20 years. He is a thoroughbred of a footballer, and an animal when he gets his dander up.

I needed to play him totally differently to Johnny Doyle or Michael Darragh Macauley. I retreated back when Kerry had possession. I sat in front of my half backs. Sometimes behind. And waited. Waited patiently until O Se took possession. Once he approached the 45 metres line I was out of my pocket and onto him. I had to meet him hard.

I didn't want him thinking that it was personal between me and him. That would not be good. If Tomas O Se thought he was fighting for his life, one last time in Croke Park, then that would not be a good thing. That was not a fight I wanted.

Better to try to kill him with kindness. Tomas O Se is not the sort of boy you want to try to intimidate.

Hands off.

No pulling him or pushing him when he was looking to get onto the ball, or had laid the ball off.

He had come up and lashed a few balls badly wide. We knew we could let them shoot from outside the 45 metres line. They might get some over, but they would not kick them all day.

Kerry ended up shooting 19 wides, compared to our six. That tells the story of the 2012 All-Ireland quarter final, and shows how good the system is when it is working. It was, however, a different Kerry to the team we would meet in the 2014 All-Ireland final.

In 2012, they did not know how to be patient. They did not know to hold onto the ball, and to only take shots at goal on their own terms.

Some of their players were shooting wildly.

They were not even set to shoot.

They were lashing the ball. Even a team as amazingly strong as Kerry, with so many star studded footballers who had won everything in the game, were lost for ideas.

We had luck on our side too.

In the seventh minute Murph was making a complete nuisance of himself as McFadden's line ball, from beneath the Cusack Stand, sailed towards the Kerry goal. There was also a sense of destiny about the goal.

It reminded us that the quarter final was our game to lose, in case we had any doubts loitering in our heads.

We didn't have any. Though it was strange to be wearing white, and equally so to have Kerry in blue. However, we got right down to business even before that goal. Murph had done enough to get in the way of their keeper Brendan Kealy, and the ball nestled in the back of the net.

Colm was on his way to scoring 1-6, in one of his near perfect performances.

Marc O Se had taken him up, but the thing about Colm is that he is so damned strong, and when he is getting lots of ball, and tuning those shoulders, he is so hard to stop. For a defender to try to rob the ball off him once he has it in his hands is twice as difficult.

We had control of the game long before it was over.

McGuinness had told us in our team meetings that we would know Kerry were in trouble when they started making substitutions before half time. In particular, he mentioned, Darran O'Sullivan. He predicted that O'Sullivan would be in before half time and that Paddy McGrath was to welcome him to the game when the time came.

And that he did. As soon as O'Sullivan entered the field in the 32nd minute he was met with an almighty shoulder from Paddy.

It was 1-4 to 0-5 at half time, and we maintained that daylight, and some more, between the teams right through the second half. McFadden's last point of the afternoon, in the 65th minute, put us 1-11 to 0-8 in front. We were home and dry.

But, at the same time, we did not go for the jugular. We never did go for the jugular in many games over McGuinness' four years, and that quarter final win was no different. That, perhaps, was the downside to our system.

We were coached to take no chances. We were coached to think that a two or three points win was all we needed.

That, and never to get caught on a counter-attack.

That was unforgivable in Jim McGuinness' book. It was ingrained in us to hold strong, and because of that we never poured forward, and never sought to totally destroy many teams on the scoreboard.

We did not push on when we were six ahead of Kerry. We retreated into our shells in defence, and manned up back there. The game looked a million miles away from becoming anything like a cliff-hanger.

Then, near disaster. We allowed, inexplicably, Donnacha Walsh to make ground on our end line. He flicked the ball across the goalmouth, and Donaghy got his big hand on it.

Paul Galvin nicked a point for them after a Colm Cooper kick looked like it was going wide. Anthony Maher followed that up with a bomb of a point, their best of the day. There was only one point in the game. They had the ball again. Paddy Curtin was in range, but he was also panicky. He had more time than he had thought, more room too.

He kicked it wide.

Papa kicked the ball out again.

It was the most important kick out of the whole afternoon. We had to win the ball. Kerry had all of the momentum. Their tails were up, and when Kerry teams believe they are about to win a game, they usually end up doing so.

The ball floated over towards Big Neil.

It broke off him, and fell nicely to me. As I took the ball in, I felt a Kerry player about to hit me. Instinctively, I felt him coming, and I swivelled around in the opposite direction.

Karlo was there.

All of our half-backs were told to get forward the minute we won possession, and Karlo was only doing what came naturally. He was racing forward, before I swivelled in his direction. At times, McGuinness wanted our men to gamble. With Eamon McGee in charge of maintaining the right number of men at the back, Karlo knew it was time to risk everything.

He had anticipated us winning the ball.

He was on my shoulder. I popped the ball off.

There was nobody at home for Kerry, because they had needed to win that kick out even more than us. They had to grab the equaliser. That's what it had come down to after 70 minutes. One kick out. One last possession. The ball could have bounced anywhere off Big Neil's hands.

It had bounced to me.

Karlo was gone.

He stroked over the last score of the game. 1-12 to 1-10.

The *Hills of Donegal* was being played in the stadium as McGuinness sent us down to the Hill 16 end of the ground to get our warm down completed. We did some light jogging. Some stretching. And the same again, and the same again, but as we did so I had a word with Murph.

He and I needed to have a word with Jim.

Karlo too. The three of us needed to talk with him in a bit of a hurry as we were flying out to London the following morning and McGuinness knew nothing about it.

We were heading over to spend 24 hours at the Olympic Games. I was due to fly out from Belfast and had arranged to stay with my sister, Tríona for the night. The two boys were flying out from Derry

In the dressing room, the two of us stood either side of Murph, or perhaps more behind him, as he stood in front of Jim.

'Listen, Jim...,' Murph began.

'We've got tickets here for the boxing in London... and the flights are got!'

'Are they... are they really?' Jim replied.

Murph nodded his head.

Karlo and I nodded as well in support.

With everything rosy in the garden, with Kerry slain, and with no pressure on anybody's shoulders for a day or two, how could Jim McGuinness genuinely say no to us?

'Aye...' said Murph, '... flights are got!'

'Alright, so ye booked to go to London,' Jim replied, '... in the middle of the championship?

We knew by his tone he was not unhappy.

We knew we were good to go. And the pair of them were waiting in a bar in Stansted the next morning, waiting for me with two cold beers in front of them. We were back in the All-Ireland semi final again. We had no worries in the world, and so much to talk about. Mostly, however, we just wanted 24 hours of complete relaxation and no talk about football.

The boys, Michael and Karl, got tickets to see some weight lifting. A group of us got tickets to the ladies' volleyball at Earl's Court. Then, the next day, I got to see Katie Taylor's semi final.

She was amazing. Not just her strength, but her hand speed, it was astonishing to witness. And the noise in the arena was deafening. The Irish had taken over the Excel Arena.

I was honoured to be there, and it never crossed my mind all day about the other boys rehabbing back at home. I never thought about Cork either. They had taken Kieran McGeeney's Kildare apart in their quarter final. It was 2-19 to 0-12 at the end. Kildare were one of the fittest team in the whole country and Cork had beaten them by 13 points.

I knew what it was like to be run over by Cork.

Conall Dunne does a great William Wallace impression, taken from the Mel Gibson movie, Braveheart. He was trying to lift our spirits as we sat around listening to quote after quote from the epic film.

Cork had just whipped us in the All Ireland quarter final in 2009. We were all in bad form as we sat in the bar but I must say listening to him was cheering me up a little.

Conall likened us to the Scots who were after being flattened by the English heavy cavalry. He wasn't far wrong. As the drink began to set in and we forgot about the match, I started enjoying the free entertainment provided by my club mate and good friend.

'I AM... WILLIAM WALLACE!'

The whole lot of us would be in tears laughing at him.

That's how we got over heavy defeats. We forgot about them and had a laugh in those days. Cork had beaten us by 14 points that day in 2009. It was 1-27 to 2-10 at the end.

I'd scored a goal. Murph kicked six points. But they had a handful of boys putting up big scores, Paul Kerrigan, Donncha O'Connor, John Miskella, Daniel Goulding, Fintan Goold. Miskella who scored four from play was my man. Enough said.

It was one of those defeats which did not need reflection.

It was the same for Dublin the next day, when they lost by 16 points to Kerry and their manager, Pat Gilroy was so completely overawed by what he had seen that he strangely volunteered his boys had looked like earwigs on the field.

We had been beaten on the Saturday night.

Dublin went down on the Sunday afternoon.

A gang of us went drinking on the Sunday night. We were still drinking on the Monday night, when we were joined by some of the Dublin boys.

Agreement to help one another drown our sorrows was easily reached. I ended up spending the night in Bernard Brogan's place in Castleknock. There were a good number of Dublin and Donegal boys there the next morning.

Back in the city centre that afternoon, Michael Boyle, Neil McGee and myself were tired drinking. We decided to eat in style.

We grabbed a Subway.

We were tucking into our rolls, half starved, as we walked down the street not knowing for sure where we were going, or what we were going to end up doing next?

'Come on...,' announced Boyler, finally. 'We're going to get the bus home!' The three of us started walking towards Busaras when, suddenly, McGee stopped in his tracks.

'I'm not getting on no bus... BOYS!'

The three of us were completely out on our feet.

A Bus Eireann ride home, stopping every 20 minutes in every town, twisting and turning forever was what awaited us. Until McGee had spoken up, and walked across the street to a taxi rank.

'Take me to Donegal, Sir!'

The African driver sitting against the front of his taxi did not say anything in reply.

'Sir... take me to Donegal...' repeated McGee.

'I can not go there!' the taxi man replied.

He did not look like a man who knew for sure where Donegal might be.

McGee told him he would be paid. The taxi man put his hand in the air.

'I have to ring my boss...

'I ring him! Okay?'

A few minutes later, he said he would indeed bring the three of us to Donegal. He said it would cost 300 euros. We paid him 280 euros.

McGee was the first to open the back door of the taxi.

'Bring me home!' he ordered as he threw himself into the back of the car.

Cork had run up the highest total ever recorded in an All-Ireland quarter final in beating us three years earlier.

Eight of us who had played against Cork in 2009 would also line out in the semi final in 2012. We did not need reminding of that catastrophe. But memories of what had happened were more personal to me than anybody else on the team. I was captain in 2009.

In nearly every interview I did in the lead up to the semi final I was being reminded of that game in 2009.

'Cork don't hold good memories for you, Rory... do they?

'How will Donegal cope with Cork's pace and physicality?'

For me, though, the difference between 2009 and 2012 was night and day.

McGuinness never mentioned the game in 2009, not once. He preferred to completely ignore it. All that concerned him was the Cork team of 2012, and he made sure that he knew that team inside out.

He told us how they were going to set up.

He told us where their scores potentially would come from. Every little thing about the Cork team was consumed by McGuinness. He could tell me exactly where their keeper, Alan Quirke would kick the ball. He had Michael Boyle, our replacement keeper kicking it just like Quirke in training. I knew exactly what to expect from Quirke. Smashing the ball down from their kick outs was therefore going to be all the easier.

Knowing our opponents inside out was always comforting, but that was McGuinness' speciality. He did not like surprises.

They had two huge men in the middle of the field, Alan O'Connor and Aidan Walsh. And Walsh was my man. He is an amazing athlete, and he scored a terrific goal against Kildare when he went bombing through the middle of their defence. That was shown to me repeatedly in the lead up to our semi final.

McGuinness warned me that so much of the Cork performance depended upon Walsh. When he went quiet, the whole team's form dipped. When he dominated the game, everyone around him lifted their performance.

The first act in preparing for Cork, however, had been to get the win over Kerry out of everyone's heads.

That was easily done.

On our first Tuesday evening back in training, McGuinness had a unique drill aimed at focusing everyone's attention. It was a simple piece of work from first glance. It looked basic enough, just two groups of us, 20 metres apart. All we had to do was come off the cone at a reasonable speed and meet one another in the middle with a handpass.

First time McGuinness always wanted it done at 80% speed, then 90% speed, then flat out. First time it's for 90 seconds, second time 60 seconds, third time 45 seconds. But, by the end of it, we always had the clearest of heads and were ready for the rest of the evening's work.

Though it is also a bit of a killer of a drill to start off a training session with, and lungs are soon burning. Everyone is flying. There's no time to think. The ball is hardly ever in anyone's hands. It all so fast, and it is all soft hands.

No ball is allowed to drop.

Everything needs to be crisp.

Smooth.

Everybody needs to be tuned in.

Once it ends, we know we are back down to business.

Next game, please!

However, as the seconds counted down to the throw up against Cork, Rory Gallagher was sprinting in different directions out on the field. Cork had moved some of their men around.

We wanted Mark McHugh on Noel O'Leary.

But O'Leary was taking up Ryan Bradley. Gallagher corrected that match up. And others. Gallagher's mission before any game commenced was to make sure that everyone was next to the man he had prepared for, and that nobody was at all distracted.

Anthony Thompson and Frank McGlynn were assigned to Paul Kerrigan and Paddy Kelly, two of their speedsters. Both of the Cork boys knew how to motor, but we were confident Tony and Frank had the legs for them.

The game was about to start.

And Gallagher was still at work on the field.

'Do you know what this is?

'This is a f****** shootout... and I'm not into shootouts!'

McGuinness was absolutely furious with us at half time. And he was especially mad that we were treating everybody in the ground to a game of football that was real end-to-end stuff, and thrilling to watch.

'F****** SHOOTOUT!'

A shootout was not in the man's DNA

McGuinness had begun the game ambitiously. Colm and Murph stayed put in our full forward line. Twin targets for a change. And therefore we were letting the ball go long more often than we had at any time all summer.

With Big Neil fetching brilliantly in the middle, and the pair of them up front, we were primed to do some damage to the Cork defence, and we did. But four times in the first half, Cork had replied to our points within 60 seconds. It was all level coming up to half time when Donncha O'Connor was hounded out of possession and we moved it down to the other end in double quick time. Karlo set up McHugh for the lead point. It was 0-8 to 0-7, and as we gathered our breath in the dressing room, Jim and Rory were hard at it outside the door, sharing their disgust with our performance.

McGuinness marched in.

There was nowhere for anybody to hide. He reared up immediately. For starters, we had no platform for our attacks!

We were not setting up in defence.

We were relying on Big Neil's fielding to set up attacks, he told us. We had no platform whatsoever. He was not yet berserk, but he was touching on it. There was so much to lose. And while we were winning the game on the scoreboard, we were losing the game in McGuinness' head.

Neil's fielding, and some joy also from turning them over had kept us in the game. Cork were also not allowing us to play the game on our terms. Fintan Goold and Paddy Kelly were pushing up on McHugh and they were not letting him play his free sweeper role. On one occasion they had intercepted the ball. Kelly got it, and tucked it over the bar.

Cork were also getting short kick outs and they were running the whole length of the field. That was doing McGuinness' head in as well. We were trying to press them up high, but they were getting through that press, and we had not got the right number of bodies back in defence. That's why they were trading scores with us so easily.

McGuinness started to do his nut about this.

There was so much that he was ready to do his nut about. But, most of all, he was horrified that we had allowed ourselves to get involved in a game that was looking more and more like a lottery.

'F****** SHOOTOUT!'

Cork had the first four attacks of the second half.

Each time they squandered a decent opportunity. We were allowing them to come up the field uncontested. We had our shape back, but we were still not putting that initial press on.

Graham Canty got on the end of the first one and kicked wide with his left, and there was a big cheer from the Donegal support that was music to our ears. Then Kerrigan kicked and hoped!

Then Sheehan shot, but the fourth time they sallied forward Big Neil got in a great block on Colm O'Neill. The ball was turned over. McFadden pointed at the other end.

We outpointed them four points to two in the third quarter. O'Neill won a ball lofted in behind our full back line, and his shot cannoned off the crossbar. Their heads dropped for a little while after that.

We were suddenly working harder than any of them. All of us were working our socks off. We were surging forward in numbers.

I played a one-two with Murph and was clean through for the first goal of the game. Anthony Thompson was inside me. I should have shot earlier, but I passed the ball off to him. And Tony gave it back to me, but the gap between me and the keeper had closed and I was not able to get my shot off.

The ball broke to Tony and he punched it over the bar. We had not hit the back of the net, but we were swarming over them. We were breaking up their attacks and turning the ball over.

Both of my calves were cramping 15 minutes from the end. I signalled to the bench for another five minutes. Quickly, I received the ball in acres on the right hand side and should have been able to point. There was nobody near me. I cramped again as I went to kick the ball. It went wide.

I left the field with 10 minutes left. I had given everything I had, as did every single soul in green and gold.

We were five points up. We had the ball. Our supporters were celebrating as the game entered injury time.

'Olé...

'Olé... Olé... Olé...

'Olé... Olé.'

We lost the ball.

O'Neill scored Cork's goal.

0-16 to 1-11, all of a sudden.

Another two points win. McGuinness was proud. We had run ourselves to a standstill. The tank was empty but we were victorious.

We were back in an All-Ireland final for the first time in 20 years. McGuinness called training for the Tuesday evening.

We were back in Ballybofey.

We were 20 yards apart from one another.

Two groups facing one another.

One ball.

'80%...!' shouted McGuinness.

'90 seconds....!

'Let's go...!'

CHAPTER 8

'There will be goals in this game!'

Over the four years I got to work with him, Jim McGuinness had an uncanny ability to predict the nature of games. He knew what our opponents would do, and often he knew when they would do it, like, for instance, when they might introduce a big substitution to try to upset the rhythm of the game. His homework on our opponents was exhaustive. At times, we all wondered where he hid his crystal ball?

We were full sure that we would be playing Dublin in the 2012 All-Ireland final, and meeting them for 'Round Two' and trying to get our revenge for the defeat in the 2011 semi final.

Instead, Mayo played like a team possessed against them. Dublin lost their grip on their All-Ireland title by 0-19 to 0-16, but at one stage in their semi final the reigning champions were 10 points behind. They threw the kitchen sink at Mayo after that and Bernard Brogan had a goal chance to save their skin, but Mayo held out, and deservedly so.

Mayo scored seven goals and 69 points in their four games in getting to the final, and they certainly packed phenomenal power at the back and in the middle of the field.

But McGuinness was not predicting that Mayo had more goals in them. He was telling us that goals would win us the All-Ireland title.

'There will be goals in this game... definitely!' he informed us.

Before we went to Johnstown House Hotel for our final camp before the final we started working to make sure his prediction was right on the money. Every night, we went to work on hitting long, diagonal balls into our full forward line.

McGuinness had decided to change his strategy for the final. He believed that Murph would be able to beat Ger Cafferkey in their full back line. He had seen enough evidence of that when we had played them in the league in Ballyshannon. As it turned out, James Horan decided to have Kevin Keane marking Murph when the ball was thrown up. Either way, we were ready to hit Murph with the most exact diagonal balls.

'We want goals... we want to hit them early with goals!' McGuinness directed every single evening.

Any time we got the ball in the Mayo half of the field, McGuinness wanted composure. Take a solo, he said. Bounce the ball, and then deliver it 40 yards diagonally into the Mayo full back line.

He wanted us aiming for the back post, but he wanted the ball landing on the edge of Mayo's large square. There, Murph had enough room, and time, to win possession and not get tangled up with a Mayo defender and their goalkeeper. He wanted Murph winning clean possession.

He wanted Murp turning with the ball.

McGuinness had us all visualise exactly what had to be done.

'Imagine the black spot on the crossbar is dissecting the pitch into two halves,' he told us. 'Imagine that line... and I want you to flight the ball diagonally just beyond that line!'

He knew Mayo would leave space at the back.

Horan was no fool, but he was a risk taker when it came to tightening up his defence sufficiently and usually left it that little bit loose.

That was Mayo's jugular.

'What are you looking for from our kickouts?' McGuinness asked.

'Are you looking at winning possession... or thinking goals?' he continued. And when we all answered possession, he shook his head.

'That's the wrong way to be thinking...

'You have to be thinking goals... from our kicks you have to be thinking goals all the time,' he insisted.

He was also telling us not to have any fear of the final.

The same promise which he repeated before every final, both Ulster finals and All-Ireland finals, was laid down in front of us.

McGuinness promised we would not lose. He told us he could see the cup sitting at the top of the bus as we were driving back to Donegal.

'The final will take care of itself...

'I GUARANTEE you that, boys!'

It was not an unhealthy level of arrogance coming from the man. He wanted us to to know that we had everything done, that we were one hundred per cent prepared. That we had put all of the work in. That we had everything covered. Therefore, we should have no doubts. We should know in our hearts that all we needed to do was to play our game.

And we would win.

Jim McGuinness and James Horan been appointed to their jobs in Donegal and Mayo at much the same time in late 2010.

The pair of them had that in common. And there was more. Jim and James also inherited two groups of footballers with a troubled past in many ways. Our biggest problem was not taking our football careers seriously enough. Theirs was losing big games.

Both Donegal and Mayo had suffered humiliations in the Qualifiers in 2010 before the two men were appointed. But Mayo had 11 boys from their bad defeat to Longford in 2010 playing in their semi final win over Dublin. We had been demolished by Armagh by nine points in 2010, but we had nine survivors from that mauling playing in our victory over Cork.

That's how far, and that's how quickly, McGuinness and Horan had brought things on.

However, they were not the best of buddies.

McGuinness had never any interest in playing challenge games against other counties. If he wanted to get things done properly in a challenge match against someone else, he was sure to be giving vital information away to a rival manager.

He preferred private training games amongst ourselves.

But, twice that rule had been broken. We played Mayo early in the summer of 2011 in Sligo after they had struggled to beat London in the first round of the championship. And we had played them again, in 2012, at the opening of a pitch in Swinford for the late Garda Robbie McCallion.

Each time, each game ended up a dogfight.

In Sligo, there were verbals from the very start, though I am not sure where this animosity between Donegal and Mayo had come from? On the bus heading down to Sligo for the game everyone was perfectly relaxed, and totally at ease and looking forward to the run out, that's all.

Minutes in, we were on the receiving end of a couple of awful late belts. The referee was trying to lay down the law, but to us, Mayo were desperate to lay down some sort of marker. For whatever reason?

It seemed to me that Horan was instilling in his team that they would never again be seen as a soft touch. He wanted a hard edge, and he wanted it every single day, every game.

I got a bad belt myself midway through the second half. I had given a fist pass and went to run on for the return, but my man had a firm hold of my jersey. He had a fistful of it. I turned around and hit him. It was instinctive. And I knew I would probably be sent off but something needed to be done.

Immediately, there was anarchy.

Everyone was involved, and some serious punches were thrown. Finally, the referee told McGuinness to take me off the field, or else he would send me off, but afterwards, in our dressing room, McGuinness spoke up for me and said I was dead right to do what I did.

'They were at it all night,' he insisted, '... and Rory was right to put a stop to it out there!'

Then, when we played them in the second challenge game earlier in 2012, the same thing started all over again. Paddy McGrath was clothes-lined. And McGuinness and Horan started at one another on the sideline.

I was injured, and I was sitting back listening to the two of them. McGuinness let him know what he thought of his team's tackling. Horan did not say as much back. He stood there with a half-smile on his face.

At half time, McGuinness called the boys into a tight huddle and ordered them to put a stop to Mayo in the second half.

The big hits continued for the next 35 minutes.

And, when we played them in the league in Ballyshannon, I had struck out at Kevin McLoughlin and got sent off. There was going to be no love lost in the 2012 All-Ireland final either, that much was certain.

It was the biggest game of my life.

I had reached the highest point of my football career. And at times like that, the low points seemed like an entirely different lifetime.

My lowest point in my life as a Donegal footballer was 2007. It was totally self-inflicted.

'Even a dog wouldn't go drinking on a Tuesday night!'

Those words were spoken by Michael Hegarty, and I never forgot them. Hegarty was talking about me and while his words hurt, all I could do was to apologise, to him and everyone on the team.

Hegarty was one of the great servants in the county. He had given everything he had for so many years and in 2011 he had played really well, and scored an important point in the Ulster final, but then he had retired. He would not get to be part of a Donegal team playing in an All-Ireland final.

We were flying in the spring of 2007, and we would end up winning the National league title for the first time in the county's history.

We had beaten Dublin by four points, and Tyrone by six, when the time came to meet the reigning All-Ireland champions, Kerry in Letterkenny. They came out of the blocks at a hundred miles per hour. They were five points up before we knew it. But we won the game by five points!

Brendan Devenney was in unstoppable form.

It was an amazing 10 points turnaround against the best team in the country, even if they didn't have Colm Cooper on board, and Kieran Donaghy had to go off after 20 minutes with a shoulder injury. We topped the Division 1A table with five wins out of five in the league.

We had a few drinks that night, but I went to work the following morning, and I was at home after having my dinner when I heard that some of our boys were still drinking in the town.

It was too late though, the lads were on a different level altogether and there was no moving them.

The following evening I got a call from a mate of mine who was having a few beers. He was wetting the head of his wee baby boy.

I decided to join him.

I never made it to training on the Tuesday evening, which was all the more crazy and ridiculous because the boys I had tried to chase out of the pub on the Monday actually made it to training on the Tuesday evening. I didn't.

I texted Brian McIver and told him I had come down with some bug, probably some kind of flu.

How did I think I'd get away with such foolishness? Looking back, it's beyond me, especially as word had already filtered back to McIver by the Tuesday evening.

Big Neil was team captain.

There were years when Big Neil had been no saint either, but he met up with me on the Wednesday and let me know exactly the size of the mess I was in. He had been getting it in the neck from Hegarty and Adrian Sweeney and some of the boys.

I phoned Brian.

I apologised, and I was expecting to be dropped from the panel. All I could say was 'sorry... sorry for letting you down!' Brian McIver was the man who had put complete trust in me, and had given me my first championship start the previous year.

And this was how I had repaid him! I never felt as low. I felt ashamed, totally, and I could sense in the phone call just how angry Brian was with my behaviour. It was not a long conversation.

'I'll see you tomorrow!'

That's all he said to me at the end.

I still thought my season was over, and that on the Thursday evening, face to face, Brian would deliver his judgment.

I went out onto the field.

Everyone was warming up, and Brian McIver had still said nothing directly to me. I called the boys in and apologised.

'I let you down...

'I'm sorry... for bringing this upon you all as a group!'

I felt two inches tall. McIver chatted with me after, and said I would get one more chance. My heart rose, and I felt a surge of determination to make the most of every hour of the rest of the season, and show Bran McIver, and all of the boys, that I was honestly and truly sorry for what I had done.

The problem was, I had let loose in the training session and I was tearing up the field soloing the ball when... POP...something went in my right quad. I didn't know what I had done? I pulled up straight away. I knew it wasn't good. A scan would later confirm the worst. A torn quad muscle. You reap what you sow I thought and I got exactly what I deserved.

We had a two point win over Kildare in the semi final. The team had a first league title in its sights. Mayo were the opposition. We both needed the title badly.

We had lost 13 finals in total since our All-Ireland win in 1992. They had the great John O'Mahony in charge, who had won two All-Irelands with Galway, and was looking to get Mayo on course for the big one!

We stayed in the Crowne Plaza Hotel in Santry the night before the game, and I tested my leg in the park at the back of the hotel the next morning with Ryan Porter, our trainer. It was still pulling on me.

There was no way I could start. But the league final ended up in an extended period of injury time, after Ciaran Bonner had been pole-axed in a collision with David Heaney. Big Neil also had to go off after a serious collision.

I was thrown in.

On my very first run up the field, the quad pulled again. I could feel it rip open. But I had to stay on the field, even if I was hobbling around the place. I was unable to run after my man. I felt perfectly useless.

It was all level, 0-10 each.

The game was into the 72nd minute when Paddy Campbell came soloing up the left side of the field. I was in the pocket in front of him, to the left of the posts, about 25 metres out from the goal. I could see him thinking of giving me the ball.

I didn't want it. I did not want the ball at all.

Please.... don't kick it in here! I silently begged him.

I was thinking of turning my back on him, to let him know for sure that there was no point kicking it to me.

But, at the last second, instinctively, I offered for the ball. It occurred to me that I might be able to pass it back to him. A one-two? Without having to actually move? But there was nobody near me when I got the ball.

I waited to get thumped. But, nothing.

It dawned on me that I was in acres of room. Paddy had stopped running, and there was nobody near me as the game had completely broken down in injury time.

Keith Higgins was running in my direction.

I had no idea what I was going to do? Higgins was now flying towards me.

I shaped to shoot with my left. I then did the worst solo dummy anyone has ever witnessed in Croke Park. The ball went high into the air. But, somehow, Higgins had bought the dummy.

He dived in thinking I was going to shoot.

The ball was back in my hands.

I had no real idea how I still had the thing. It was all mental. Everything seemed to be happening in slow motion.

I've still got it, I told myself.

I have to do something.

I was on my right side, and I was wondering to myself would I have the power in my leg, with my right quad ripped, to be able to kick the thing over the bar from 25 metres?

My momentum and my body position left me with no choice. If I was going to kick the ball, it had to be with my right foot. I gave it everything.

The ball crept over the bar, barely, miraculously.

We were one point up.

Eamon McGee, another substitute, put us two up in the 74th minute. Three minutes later, with the referee still not blowing it up, another of our substitutes, Adrian Sweeney made it 0-13 to 0-10. Our first league title.

We had played in three losing league finals since the glory of 1992. The joy of finally landing a big win in Croke Park was amazing, and McIver gave the team the whole week off. For me, however, the dark cloud from March had never lifted. Brian and Adrian McGuckian, his assistant, had been so decent to me. I had seen lads booted off the panel for a whole year for less.

Brian had allowed me to be part of an historic day. And a few weeks down the road he personally drove me to Belfast to get more attention for my quad injury which continued to persist. He was a total gentleman to me.

● ● ●

I owed Brian McIver so much, and could do so little for him in 2007, as our summer fizzled out in complete disappointment. We had beaten Armagh by a point in the first round of the championship, which was another huge day, and another historic victory, But we lost by 11 points to Tyrone in the semi final in Ulster. I was back on the team and playing well thanks to Brian McIver's extra care and attention, and I would have done anything to help him become the most successful Donegal manager ever.

We beat Leitrim by two points in the Qualifiers after extra time, then we beat Westmeath by five. But we lost to Monaghan by eight in our next game. I scored a goal and two points. But it wasn't enough.

It wasn't nearly enough to save my year and make it any way memorable. After that defeat McIver resigned, and then had a re-think. He was forced to interview for the job, and got one more year, getting the nod of approval over Charlie Mulgrew and Jim McGuinness.

We didn't know too much about McGuinness' intentions, and only read about him in the papers. Most of the talk was about the possible management pairing of Charlie Mulgrew and Declan Bonner. Though we all wanted McIver to stay on. But 2008 ended up a nonentity of a year.

We lost to Derry by two points in the first round. In round two of the Qualifiers we went down to Monagan again, this time by a single point. In the middle of the summer, in one newspaper interview, Eamon McGee mentioned that perhaps the Donegal team needed more than a manager.

'We probably need a sports psychologist,' said Eamon, '... as much as a football trainer.'

Prophetic words indeed.

Aidan O'Shea was one of four or five Mayo players we had identified for closer treatment. McGuinness handed him to me.

But we were in disagreement about how I would take O'Shea and also get into my defensive position all of the time. I told Jim on this occasion that I could not do both.

O'Shea is such a big player for them.

I did not want him being on one of those big runs of his just as he was on our doorstep, right on the 45 metres line. He was someone I needed to get closer to further out the field, the minute he got onto the ball.

Not 15 or 20 seconds later.

If O'Shea was coming at full belt when he hit our 45 meters line he was going to be very hard to stop. My plan was to play more side by side with him, and stop him getting the ball if at all possible in the first instance.

McGuinness and I talked it over and over in the weeks before the game, and we struggled to land on the same page. He wanted me picking up O'Shea out the field, but also finding my place back in defence when O'Shea did not have the ball. He wanted me doing both. Handling O'Shea and also working like a dog. I thought that was a huge risk.

'You either want me in the defensive line...

'Or... you want me going man to man?' I insisted.

I wanted clarity.

There had to be a choice.

I had a real problem visualising in my own mind doing both things. In the end, once the game began, I relied on instinct.

At times I felt I had to go man to man and tangle with him. Other times, when he was involved early on and laid the ball off, I got back to my position in our defensive system. If he seemed to have dropped out of their offensive play I immediately sprinted back to my position.

I did not think for one second that I would be coming off second best to him. But, tangling with him was easier said than done. He is a big man, and I reckoned he had at least a two stones advantage on me. Grappling with him would be a fool's decision. That meant I had to pressure him when we had the ball. I knew there were areas of his game that I could exploit. I was never going to go shoulder to shoulder, or try to push him around as I had done with other boys, but I knew he could not live with me if I started running around the ground. And I also knew that if I challenged behind him in the air and smashed the ball down he would begin to have creeping doubts.

I wanted to try and kick an early score.

That would be a slap on the jaw for him. And, I did start off the game well, and while I did not get my point, I set up Mark McHugh for one when I took a ball out of defence and made the transition to attack. I also got a clean fetch early on.

Most importantly of all, we got the goals we wanted.

Two of them.

Each came right out of the playbook we had been running in training between the semi final and the final. And there could easily have been a third in the space of the first 15 minutes of the game, if McFadden had not slipped. That would have left the game over and out, but their keeper saved the shot as Colm lost his footing. It was all so perfect.

And that spelled trouble for me.

The more the game went on, the more I started thinking... *We have this now... this game is ours!* And less about the process of winning the game... where I needed to be on the field? What I needed to do?

We're hammering the shite out of these boys!

That was just one thought that parachuted into my head.

I was beginning to enjoy the game.

I immediately realised that this should not be, and I tried my best to shut my brain down.

Whoa... whoa, whoa, whoa!

You're slipping.

You're not thinking

Get back into it... think, think!

I was talking to myself.

Reprimanding myself mostly. But the struggle in my head continued, and Mayo also started to come back at us on the scoreboard.

It was one f****** foot pass that started my head spinning.

It was nothing to do with Aidan O'Shea.

Negatives were starting to creep into my mind.

I needed to reboot my brain.

But that one foot pass, that I had misdirected and went out over the sideline, would not leave me alone.

Murph and McFadden produced the goods when it really mattered.

They ended the All-Ireland final with 2-8 between them, including three frees each. We were surprised to see Kevin Keane on Murph. After watching his full back struggle with Murph in our league meeting in Ballybofey James Horan had doubts about Cafferkey that did not go away. We were full sure it would be Cafferkey. Murph was too big for Keane, far too strong.

It was 2-1 to 0-0 after 11 minutes.

It was the best possible start in the world.

And, also, the worst!

How do you beat a start like that?

What do you do after it?

Murph had fired home his sensational goal after three minutes. It was a thunderbolt. It was a goal that not just registered on the scoreboard, but knocked the stuffing out of their whole defence. Colm banged in the second.

Horan switched Cafferkey onto Murph, but the damage had been done, just as we had planned. However, we had not planned for a second quarter that was the flip side of the first.

We began to turn over some soft ball. Our kicking became too risky, we were trying to force the ball inside. We also wasted chances to stretch our lead. There was Colm's second goal chance, and then straight after that Murph was short with a fisted effort at a point.

Mayo finally got on the scoreboard in the 16th minute.

We knew they would score sometime, but when opponents finally land a score after such a long wait, sometimes it can feel a heavier blow than it should be for the winning team. So, their first point hit us harder in the midrift than it should have, and before we knew it we were heading in at half time with only a three points lead. It was 2-4 to 0-7, and not such an impressive total from us after the start we had given ourselves.

Two of their points, from Michael Conroy and Enda Varley were also of the miracle variety, and really hurt us. But clearly those same two wonder scores lifted them. They had tried to really impose themselves on the game at the start, and as we expected, they put in some big hits. That was down to Cian O'Neill, their trainer, who had clearly been trying to make them a stronger, meaner team all year. Their discipline was poor, however, and they picked up some bookings early on.

It was only when Mayo fell back into their rhythm and began to play football, that they also got into the game.

Mayo's full forward line would end the game with eight points only between them. Conroy and Varley got their brilliant pair, but there was no more from Conroy after that. Varley only got a second point from a free kick, and their ace marksman, Cillian O'Connor on whom they depended so heavily finished up with five points from his afternoon's work. But, crucially, all of these were from frees, none from open play.

Our full back line was that good. Neil and Eamon McGee, and Paddy McGrath, were outstanding.

Neil and Eamon I seemed to have known all of my life, and they are two such different personalities, though both carry a reputation for not taking prisoners and are proud of that.

Eamon is more of a thinker about the game than Neil. His personality is quirky. He likes his comic books, for instance, but he would have very high standards for himself and that would leave him ultra critical at times of his own performances.

Eamon made his 100th appearance for Donegal in the final. But, he was somewhat fortunate to be anywhere near the field, as he did not buy into what Jim McGuinness had to offer at the very beginning. He was not around when it all began.

'He'll not be able to turn some boys!' I'd hear people say that, some of these people my friends in Letterkenny.

And people had every right to be sceptical.

But, how wrong anybody was to doubt the McGees. In the four years with McGuinness, I saw Neil McGee go to a completely new level. He was awesome to watch. Strength, pace and power. Nobody came close to him.

And I knew Eamon so well all the way up. We are close friends and have been for many years. We see a lot more of each other now that he is living and working in Letterkenny. Since Zoe has arrived he probably gets asked to do more babysitting than he would like, but nonetheless Zoe loves having him around. Eamon has a big heart and is one of those really generous fellas.

Often enough, I had spent the night in their home in Gweedore. Their mother, Ann is an amazing woman, and a truly generous hostess. How proud she was to have her three men, Eamon, Neil and Peter (who is the biggest and the most civil of the three of them!) on the Donegal squad in 2012.

In club games, however, neither Eamon nor Neil would spare me if they got half a chance. If they got the ball, they would be happy. But if they got the ball and the man, they would be happier still.

When I arrive with St Eunan's in Maghergallon to play Gaoth Dobhair there is never any holding back. And the home support don't hold back either as I discovered once in a club league game. I was only back from a five month trip around the world, which included Australia.

I got sent off for fighting with their corner back Sean MacGarbheith. As I was making my way out the gate toward the dressing room, I noticed an old man standing leaning over a small white wall.

'Kavanagh', he shouted.

'You should've stayed in Australia... ya bollix!'

Eamon had a good chuckle to himself afterwards when I told him what this fella had said to me. 'Did you expect anything less?' he said.

Welcome home.

He was right... this was home. The away days in Magheragallon. The 'townies' versus 'na fir Gaeltachta'. Two proud clubs coming together to do battle. I enjoyed our battles and I think the respect was mutual.

Eamon would lash out when he wanted to, but his genius lay in being a master of the darker side of the game. The pair of them are brilliant footballers, and in McGuinness' years their discipline was extraordinary. They were experts at looking to start all-out war, and at the same time staying cool as a breeze.

I knew in my heart, from the start to the very end of the 2012 All-Ireland final, that we would not be let down by the McGees.

It was an impossibility.

If there was a ball which one hundred per cent needed to be won, one of them would win it. If there was a race to a dirty ball that needed one hundred per cent to be claimed, it would be theirs.

All day long.

My problem had started midway through the first half when I got a ball from Papa under the Hogan Stand, and took it, and saw McHugh 20 yards away from me. I should have fisted it to him.

Instead, I kicked it.

It skewered off my boot. Quickly, they went up the other end and they almost scored.

I was pissed with myself and my decision making. And, then, something happened. I began to analyse everything I was doing.

And over analysing.

I was a bit like a golfer who misses a three foot putt. The next time he putts from a short distance he is talking to himself, and telling himself not to f*** it up again, and he begins to take far too much care. He over thinks.

I started to battle with myself every time I was on the ball.

The conversation did not stop.

For the rest of the game, I was talking to myself, shouting at myself, reassuring myself, and could not shut up.

Keep it simple.

Don't give it away.

I might have a man 20 yards in front of me.

Hit is softly.

Keep this pass on line.

I had tried to connect with Murph with a couple of long balls in the first half, but McGuinness did not like that I was kicking too far out the field. He had a right go at me during the game, and again at half time.

I had kicked one from 60 metres out.

I was out of range.

He had coached us to kick it in from 40 metres or so, diagonally, right across the imaginary black line running down the middle of the field. One kick I had made right in front of Jim.

The ball was intercepted.

'Gameplan.... GAME...PLAN!'

He was roaring at me.

'GAME... PLLAAANNNNNN.'

In the dressing room at half time, McGuinness told us what we needed to hear, straight up.

He told us we thought the game was over.

He told us were looking at the finishing line.

He told us all that we were no longer playing as we had planned, and that if we did not get back to our gameplan we would lose the All-Ireland final.

He told us we were taking the wrong options on the ball.

Before the game, as we left our dressing room, he had told us that we were going to produce the perfect team performance in the All-Ireland final.

Our perfection had lasted for 11 minutes.

But McGuinness was calm. He told us we were making basic mistakes. He told us, as he told us a dozen times in training sessions, that one mistake leads to a second mistake. One man messes up, then the man behind him is probably going to mess up also. It's a domino effect.

That's what he told us was happening out on the field in the second quarter. But, he was speaking quietly, and deliberately. There was no trace of anger in his face, or his voice.

'Throw the heads back, boys!'

That's what he always wanted us to do when he needed us to take in everything he was saying.

We were sitting there, eyes closed, heads back, and there was now total silence. All talk had stopped.

We had been in Johnstown House Hotel the night before.

On the Friday night I had been down with my mother and father. There was a Blessed Candle already doing its work on the kitchen windowsill. Mum was worrying over me. Dad had few words, just a firm handshake and a request to do the business on the big day.

McGuinness left it up to ourselves whether we stayed in Johnstown House or Carton House in Kildare the night before the final. Johnstown was always that bit more homely.

We were sleeping in the chalets at the rear of the hotel. Myself and Big Neil were together, as usual, and we had Paddy McBrearty as our special house guest! We made him welcome by hiding his stuff, his bag, toiletries, anything we could get our hands on.

Our team talk had been short enough, about an hour, and we had watched clips of Mayo beating Dublin again. We had a good look and talk about the boys we were targetting... Vaughan, Keegan, O'Shea.

And Cillian O'Connor. Mayo did not have men like The Gooch or Bernard Brogan. O'Connor was still up and coming. Alan Dillon was such a strong heartbeat for them, but we felt Karlo could do a job on him.

We relaxed for a little while. There was a pool table, a dart board, table tennis, X-Box in our team room. Everyone was excited, but ready for bed. We were then served up our team's most important tradition. The freshly baked scones and cream arrived, with a variety of jam, and were scoffed.

I had a great night's sleep.

I called Kathryn first. She had given me a card, and also gave me clear instructions not to open it until the morning of the game.

I needed to open it on Saturday night.

I did not want any distractions on the Sunday morning. I wanted my mind totally clear. So, I was sitting on the edge of my bed on Saturday night, with Kathryn's card beside me.

On the phone I had asked her if I could open it?

'No!' she replied, firmly.

I put in my iPod and lay back, and waited for a drowsiness to creep over me. I did not have to wait long. I turned the music off. That's all I remember. The next morning I ripped open the card.

I still wanted to protect my clear head.

Kathryn had chosen her words perfectly, and she included a brilliantly chosen quote... 'The future belongs to those who believe in the beauty of their dreams...'

This is it.

This is... it, I told myself.

My head was filled with positive thoughts. You ain't gonna lose this one I told myself as I made my way across to the hotel for breakfast where I joined Big Neil who was already at the table.

Myself and Big Neil liked our match day routine on away days.

Whether it was a league game or the morning of the All Ireland final, it didn't matter. After breakfast, one of us would usually grab The Sunday Independent in the hotel reception and head to the room. I usually liked to flick through the small Life magazine that accompanies the paper, while Neil flicked through the sports section.

The Life magazine had little bits of everything in it from showbiz and celebrity gossip to cooking, but they usually did an in-depth interview with someone interesting which I liked to read. It's a million miles away from what we were about to encounter on the pitch but I welcomed the distraction for a brief while.

One particular interview was with Rosanna Davidson and she was talking about her German Playboy shoot. She was giving her reasons for doing the nude shoot in the first place as she had come in for some criticism from certain quarters.

After a brief discussion both myself and Big Neil agreed she was dead right to do what she did given the amount of money that was involved.

We would then chat about a few of the celebrities that appeared in the pictures on the first few pages of the magazine. It wasn't just Rosanna, we would cast our opinion on them all.

'What you think of that Ryan Gosling fella... Neil?' I would say

'Tube,' would be the reply.

'Why?' I asked. 'He's a decent actor!'

'Nah, useless.'

'What about this Pippa O'Connor... what do you think of her?'

'Aye , she's not bad... but I'd prefer that Nadia Forde one.'

The banter passed the morning for us.

And we usually squeezed in a wee nap too.

The hours flew by.

We were on the field, as McGuinness had meticulously planned, 40 minutes before the game began. We had our warm ups and our drills, and he ensured we were reminded all through what awaited each and every one of us. He did not want anyone forgetting the gameplan.

As we met the President of Ireland, and all of the dignitaries, he had also put in action a plan to keep our minds on the business to come.

We all had coaching points, lines he asked us to use to prompt one another as we waited around and looked around. As Michael D Higgins walked and talked to us, we all kept prompting one another, non stop.

Same in the parade.

The man behind kept prompting.

Whatever happened, we were not going to lose our gameplan once the game began. But even Jim McGuinness had been unable to prevent that from happening after our blistering start.

We had scored our goals.

Mayo had come back at us. We had our reality check. We did not expect any more goals, we did not think we would get anything easy in the second half.

We awaited a long, gruelling 35 minutes. Mayo had not crumbled, as they had done in the past in All-Ireland finals. They had stood up to us. They had come back at us with a definite intention.

We needed to run the ball better.

The long ball into Murph was unlikely to be on anymore, but if we got the chance to isolate him, then perhaps we might get a third goal. But we did not expect one. We had our three points advantage.

We had to protect that first of all.

They were cynical in the tackle, but that suited us. Free kicks would win us the All-Ireland, just as certainly as another goal or two.

We maintained daylight between us and them. Our lead moved from three to four, and then to five points, and then came back down to three points again, but they were not producing any ace.

Christy Toye came in and added extra energy to everything we did with his running power. I set up Murph and he slapped over for a point at the Davin End. It could've gone anywhere.

Murph fisted our second last point.

They had got no goals.

No ace.

Big Neil banged over our final score.

The last five minutes dragged. The stewards had come out and started forming their shields around the ground. It was hard not to notice them. And seeing them made the wait for the final whistle even more intense.

Not long left.

Four minutes.

It's got to be over.

Any second... next ball that goes out?

Three.

I was willing myself not to look up at the clock on the scoreboard. It suddenly dawned on me there might be seven or eight minutes left?

Concentrate!

Two minutes. And still no ace from Mayo, but they still appeared to have all of the time in the world. It felt like the game was stretching out forever.

It's got to be over... maybe it's not?

Don't look up.

One minute.

Donegal 2-11, Mayo 0-13.

Cavan, Derry, Tyrone, Down, Kerry, Cork and Mayo.

We were All-Ireland champions

I had half expected a pitch invasion.

Like 1992 when I sat at home with my mother and watched Donegal winning a first All-Ireland.

I started running around the ground. I wanted to find Kathryn... my mother and father.

Alan Dillon and I were very good friends from our Sigerson Cup days in Maynooth. He'd lost his third senior All-Ireland final. He'd lost at minor. He'd lost at Under-21. I felt for him and went looking for him. There wasn't much I could say.

What do you say? All I could do was shake Alan's hand and throw my arm around him.

There was music blaring.

Streamers were turning the field into a street carnival.

I could not see Kathryn anywhere.

We made a big run down to the Hill 16. The only familiar faces I picked out the whole way around the pitch was Kathryn's sister, Liesel and her husband, Sean who were in the Cusack Stand. We exchanged a big thumbs up. It was nice to see them.

And, then, I was sitting halfway up the steps of the Hogan Stand. I was exhausted. I was breathing in every second, and trying to make out that the moment is for real. That it's over.

Aidan O'Shea was done with. Mayo were done with. Murph was waiting a few yards away from me, and the Sam Maguire was right there beside him.

A moment later, he was holding it high.

I had embraced McGuinness down under the Hill.

'We've done it!' he told me.

We held each other tightly. At the Hogan Stand, Michael Murphy stretched his hand out to Liam O'Neill, Uachtarán Cumann Lúthchleas Gael.

'Sorry to hear about your sister, Liam,' Murphy said. 'I really am.'

O'Neill's sister, Barbara had succumbed to a long illness in England the day before.

Murph, as he would, had prepared the speech. As it drew to a close, he said there was one more thing and he burst into song. *Jimmy's Winning Matches* had become a familiar anthem that summer, having been composed on the beach in Lanzarote by Rory Gallagher. The words reverberated around Croke Park.

Word had it that Paddy Power offered 16/1 on the song being part of the victorious captain's speech. Generous Paddy.

Very generous!!

Back in the dressing room, everyone was hugging and high-fiving, and there were smiles aplenty as the cameras came out. Soon, it quietened a little and everyone just sat down. It was time to take it all in.

The changing room has little dividers, almost like booths which separate each player. I just laid my head back and there it was, right in front of my eyes, sitting in the middle of the room in almost complete silence... the Sam Maguire.

On the Hogan Stand Murph, as he was about to lift the trophy, had said...
'We have him!'

Our banquet in The Burlington Hotel was an amazing night spent with
family, friends and team mates. I had waited for hours and hours after the
game to finally see my family. When I got to grips with my Dad, at last, the
satisfaction on his face and the tears in his eyes, overwhelmed me.

It was the most powerful moment of all for me.

I felt that I had delivered something for my father. Winning the All-Ireland
could not be compared to the birth of Zoe. That moment was a thousand
times more emotional. A million times more overwhelming.

But I felt all the same that I had handed something that money could not
buy to my mother and father, and my family. I had brought them Sam.

If my football career had ended, there and then, I imagined the conclusion
absolutely inch perfect.

On Monday afternoon, the rain fell in sheets as we turned out of The
Burlington Hotel and headed for home.

Sam was at the front of the bus.

As Jim McGuinness had promised us it would be.

They reckoned 25,000 people turned up in Donegal town on the Monday
night to welcome us home with Sam.

It took 25 minutes for us all to make it from Flood's Garage to the
Diamond in the town centre. A group of stewards, linked arm in arm, led us
foot by foot through the throng, the pipe band behind them, until our team
bus finally pulled up. Daniel O'Donnell joined us on stage.

'Somebody told me that Jim McGuinness does a rare version of *Destination
Donegal*,' Daniel announced, as the raindrops crackled off the green and gold
umbrellas. Although initially a touch reluctant, McGuinness made his way
to the front of the stage.

'Holy mother of God,' he began, as he grasped the microphone.

But McGuinness was more than able to hold a note.

In the days that followed every town and village that had once housed one of us was visited. On the Thursday night the final port of call was Glenswilly, Murph's home club. We'd travelled 867 kilometres, through 40 towns and villages.

In between stops, there was plenty happening.

At one stage, McGuinness came halfway down the bus to survey the damage.

'We need to get these boys some food,' he said.

'Half of them are sideways.'

From the back of the bus, in an increasingly high-pitched tone came:

'WE NEED MORE BEER!'

It was Frank McGlynn's voice and the more he drank the higher his voice got. The shout would go up... 'WE NEED MORE BEER!'

Followed by the roar of laughter.

'Shut up Frank!' came the reply from the top of the bus and there would be more laughing.

Pettigo, as always, was precious. As was a quick stop with my 97 year old Grandmother, Susan in her home in Convoy. She looked surprised when myself and Michael Murphy strode in holding the cup.

'God!' she exclaimed. 'Who's this?'

'This is Michael Murphy with the Sam Maguire Granny,' I said.

'Yiz did well then,' she said.

'We did Granny... we did!'

There's a picture of Granny and Grandad holding the Sam Maguire cup back in 1992. It was taken in their front room of the house. It was a special moment being able to bring Sam back to the same house after 20 years.

By and large, laughter and good spirits filled the bus for those four long days. But Ardara will always stick with me. It had been a tough year in Ardara after Martina Maguire, who would've been 17 that very day we landed with Sam, died of cancer in January.

Then, in June, her cousin, 24-year-old Tomas Maguire, who was offered a place on McGuinness' panel, was killed in Australia. Paddy McGrath was

Maguire's closest friend.

'Martina would've been here with her beautiful smile to welcome home the team,' MC Paddy McGill said. 'We think of her cousin Tomas, who was a legend. Their families and the club would like to thank Jim and the panel for recognising their memories.'

Paddy McGrath came into his hometown on the back of a green and gold van as bonfires burned on the roadside. Anthony Molloy, another famous Ardara man, had captained Donegal in 1992 and taken Sam to the town. Now it was Paddy's turn.

From the stage, he spoke from the bottom of his heart. It was typical Paddy, honest to the core.

Through those few days we also made it to Michael Boyle's Termon, where 24-year-old Andrew Duffy had played. Andrew lost his life after Donegal beat Cork in the All-Ireland semi final, in the Royal Canal near Binn's Bridge in Phibsboro.

'A young man went to support us but never came home,' McGuinness said. 'It would be remiss of me not to mention him as sadly it's something we're all familiar with. I'm happy we were able to bring the cup back in his memory.'

In Letterkenny on the Tuesday evening, I felt speechless. I was welcomed on stage with Kevin Rafferty but not before we posed for a brief photo with my God-daughter, Aoife (my sister, Una's daughter) who was placed into the Sam Maguire. To see so many familiar faces in the crowd all waving and smiling made me feel 10 feet tall. I felt like I was sharing the moment with everyone who had ever helped me get to that moment in my career. Kevin and I were both St Eunan's men to the core and seeing all of our great club members in front of us was brilliant.

'You may search the whole world over
But no equal can be found,
to the place where I was born and bred
Sweet Letterkenny town!'

Letterkenny was certainly sweet that night, and when morning did arrive, we took the cup to my school. The principal, Paraig Cannon and the rest of the staff at Scoil Cholmcille welcomed us with open arms. The principal and staff had been such a support to me in the days and weeks leading up the final. Joe Crossan, my teaching colleague, even went to the bother of writing a poem about our journey.

We have a proud tradition of football in the school and the boys themselves are the best in the world. I attended the school as a young boy and I can only imagine how I would've felt if I got a chance to see the Sam up close and personal. There was a huge roar when I entered the backyard with Kevin Rafferty, Frank McGlynn, and Colm Mc Fadden. It was deafening and I was especially delighted for all the boys.

Afterwards, we made our way up to St Eunan's College where Colm teaches, and he took us through the hallowed corridors into the study hall. It was a proud day for us and for the likes of Neil Gordon, who alongside Paddy Tunney had managed our school teams when we studied there.

It was two o'clock on Wednesday morning when Jim McGuinness finally landed back home in Glenties with his team, and with Sam.

At that stage I was officially burnt out partying. There had been no let up from Sunday evening. Myself and Kathryn went to get a burger and chips at 3.30 am. Barely able to keep our eyes open any longer we went to bed in the Highland Hotel in Glenties.

Kathryn was up for work the next morning at 8.0 am. I could barley lift my head off the pillow to say goodbye to her. As she was about to leave the room, in burst Eamon McGee and collapsed onto the bed beside me.

He grunted something that sounded like a line from a Guns n Roses song, then fell into a deep sleep. Kathryn shook her head and off she went, neither having the time nor the patience to deal with any of this now.

In October, however, the Allstar award winners were announced. And Donegal received eight.

Eight Donegal men were handed the highest individual honours in the game, and the rest of us were, for all intents and purposes, told to try again.

That's a fact of life in football.

Every team that wins an All-Ireland title is divided down the middle by the end of the year, and there are those who get their prized statuettes, and those who are considered and thought not to be worthy enough. And it hurts. I did not expect it to hurt at all as I walked away from Croke Park a month earlier. Nor in the days that followed, did I or anyone else give a damn.

But, one month later, when you do not get an Allstar award, it is surprisingly disappointing. I felt that I had done enough. Myself and Big Neil had talked it over once or twice with Eamon McGee, wondering who'd get one, who would not? I told the pair of them that unless I was chosen for one of the forward positions that Big Neil was going to be Donegal's chosen midfielder.

I fully believed that, and understood how the Allstar selection committee always works. A pair of midfielders from a winning All-Ireland team never get recognised together.

I knew it was to be Big Neil after his performance against Cork, but I did feel that I had done more than Aidan Walsh from Cork, who was named as his midfield partner. It was Walsh's second. I had handled Walsh and every man I had played on, right up to Aidan O'Shea in the All-Ireland final.

I was delighted for all of our boys who got their awards, for Papa, Neil McGee, Karlo and Frank in the half back line, Big Neil, McHugh, Murph and Colm up front.

It's a selfish game at heart. Football, they say, is a team game and that there is 'no i in team', but that's not strictly true. Everyone has to be bloodthirsty in their own right to be the best they can be, and that is what makes a team.

We could be proud. How many times will Donegal ever get all three nominations for the Footballer of the Year award? Karlo, Frank and Colm were all shortlisted.

For me, Karlo is perhaps the most complete defender ever to have worn a Donegal shirt. Frank had an unbelievable season from start to finish, but we would never have won the All-Ireland title without Colm.

All of my energy had transferred to my club straight after the All-Ireland final.

We spent the next few weeks winning the county title again, beating Glenties. We were lucky. Halfway through the second half we trailed 0-8 to 0-5. It was our sixth championship outing in five weeks, with the first of those coming exactly a week after the All-Ireland final.

Daragh Gallagher, in particular, was outstanding and but for a save from our goalkeeper, John Paul Clarke in a one-on-one with Leo McLoone, we might've been gone.

We scraped back level through a goal from Lee McMonagle and it was level with seconds left.

Bizarrely, we were awarded a 45 after Brendan McDyer took a quick line ball back to his goalkeeper, Stephen McGrath, who wasn't on the same wavelength and the ball went wide.

Confusion reigned but a 45 was awarded. Mark McGowan, who had developed a knack that summer from placed balls, drilled it over the crossbar. We won by a point, 1-7 to 0-9.

And that, for me, was everything. It was also something much more, because St Eunan's won the league and championship. I had also won a Railway Cup medal with Ulster in 2012, and I had lived the ultimate dream of being part of Jim McGuinness' team and he had, as promised, filled my pockets with medals. Two more in 2012, an Ulster medal and an All-Ireland medal.

I was not an Allstar in 2012, but I was the first Donegal footballer to win all five of these titles in the one year.

How lucky was I?

I had received a text message from Eamon McGee to tell me who had been named on the Allstar team for 2012. And when Jim McGuinness was suddenly big news in early November, I again heard it unofficially, on the internet, like the rest of the country.

McGuinness had joined Glasgow Celtic in a full-time professional capacity as the club's Performance Consultant.

The news got everyone talking. Wondering, and whispering.

Worrying.

Is this man going to be able to commit to us as well? We were all talking, all of the team. What is going to happen now with this man?

Is he going to travel over and back?

It can't be the same?

Every one of us was so happy for him, and wished him the very best. But there was not a Donegal footballer who did not fear the worst for himself.

What about us?

I did not see McGuinness until the presentation of our medals in the Mount Errigal Hotel in Letterkenny.

Life after the All-Ireland final had been mental. The boys were travelling all over the place, covering every inch of the county, morning, noon and night. As they did so, I spent eight weeks solid with St Eunan's.

The team had not met up officially.

There was no sit down, no evaluation. The All-Ireland final, in all its perfection early on, its failure midway through, and its businesslike finish, was left to rest.

A good number of the squad decided to meet in the Swilly Inn pub in Letterkenny before going out to our medal presentation in the Mount Errigal Hotel.

'How's it going?' I asked Jim.

McGuinness told me it was brilliant with Celtic, and he took me through his whole routine, how he was working with their young players and looking to make a vital difference in their careers.

'I am still going to commit to you!' he assured me.

'Do not worry...

'I will not miss one training session!'

And McGuinness never did miss a single session in 2013 or 2014. Colm McFadden's father, Colm Snr picked him up and dropped him off at the airport every single time.

Even his time keeping remained meticulous.

He surprised us all again.

Jimmy Tunes?

Who was that man?

2013

CHAPTER 9

We celebrated the arrival of the New Year in Dubai.

The Sandance Party was a New Year's Eve celebration on the beach at Atlantis on the Jumeirah Palm. It was a million miles removed from Castlefin on a wet morning in January. My season had been extended by some eight or nine weeks with St Eunan's. After beating Glenties in the final we exited for the second time in the Ulster club championship at the hands of Crossmaglen in the Athletic Grounds in Armagh. We played poorly, much different to our meeting in 2008 when we almost toppled them in Brewster Park.

Dubai was a welcome treat after a long but fruitful season. And we were in the expert hands of Seamus Byrne, an Ardara native who was living out there. I'd always said that the people from Ardara were a good sort, and Seamus was the very best. His kindness and generosity knew no bounds.

We lived it up, as All-Ireland winners do and forgot completely about what awaited us when we got home. One of the many highlights was our night at the luxurious Meydan racecourse, with its one kilometre long finishing stretch. As special guests, we were asked to do one of the presentations.

Myself and a few of the lads accepted the role of team ambassadors. We were in direct view of the television cameras, and while we waited for the winning jockey and owners and local dignitaries to arrive, my phone in the breast pocket of my jacket would not stop vibrating.

I was getting call after call. Text messages were bombing in! I ignored them all, and myself and the others did what we had to do.

Once the job was over with, I grabbed for my phone.

'You should not be chewing gum on television!'

All of the calls and texts were from Raymond Blake and all of the boys in Blake's Bar in Letterkenny. Blake's is the St Eunan's haunt, where post-match dissections usually take place. They were watching the races.

'Should have taken the gum out of your mouth... Rory!'

We had nothing much done.

Back at home, the year looked a long stretch ahead of us, but we realised that we were going to be playing catch up for a few months at least. There had been gym work organised in the autumn after winning the All-Ireland, but with all of the activities and demands being placed on everyone, that fell by the wayside now and again.

The Sam Maguire Cup was on tour to every nook and cranny of the county. Two of my sisters got married in 2012. First up was Donna. She married in October. I managed to get my hands on Sam for a surprise visit to the post wedding party in the Harbour Bar, Downings. Her husband Pat, is a Mayo man so there was a good bit of slagging done after the final in 2012. Donna and Pat had no idea that I jumped into a taxi and had gone to Termon in the middle of the night to bring the cup back to the pub in Downings. A great night just got even better when Sam arrived in through the door. The celebrations went on long into the night as both sets of families and friends partied with Donna and Pat.

Sam made its second official visit to a Kavanagh family celebration in December. Another sister, Alma married a Teelin man, Seamus Curran. I swear to God, it was like both of them knew that Donegal would be champions in 2012. Alma is the organiser in chief of all things GAA-related in our family. She is a school principal by profession so I guess she has to be. Alma, being as organised as ever, made sure that Sam was booked for her big day and was placed proudly near the top table for all to see.

In Dubai we had tried to do a little bit of training.

McGuinness was of a mind to just do a couple of sessions. I'm not sure why?

The first session came the morning after a completely mad night out. Jim obviously thought it a good idea, but it was one of his worst. We did not get to our beds until after four in the morning.

The phone next to my bed started ringing, continuously, and it seemed that we had just shut our eyes so Kathryn and I completely ignored it.

But, it would not stop.

'There's something up...

'You'd better answer it!' Kathryn told me.

'No... no, no... it's alright!' I replied, groggily, rolling over for another couple of hours. The ringing continued, then stopped.

Then started again.

Kathryn finally grabbed the damn thing.

'WHAT...?' she asked, though it was more of a bark.

'Kathryn?

'Jim here...!' said McGuinness.

'Oh, sorry Jim...' replied my loving wife, with her tone of voice lowered in double quick time.

'Is Rory there?'

'He's lying here, yeah... fast asleep!'

'Would you tell him,' McGuinness continued,'... would you tell him that all of the boys are down here at reception... waiting for him.'

'I will Jim... thanks Jim!'

While Kathryn was being nice as pie to Jim, I was muttering to myself and trying to work my legs out of the bed.

F*** sake...

What is he doing... what time is it?

On the beach, all of us were quickly dying. We had been warned that there would be a couple of sessions, and we had all of our gear, but our heads weren't right. Our bodies were wrecked.

The sweat was pouring out of us after the first couple of runs. Then we did some sprints. It was crazy stuff, and to cap it all I stretched my groin trying to run faster than my body was interested in allowing me to run.

It was good to be home. It was something special to be running out onto the pitch and being clapped by the opposition. But the novelty of this situation quickly wore off, and the reality set in, in double quick time.

We are the men!

We're the top dogs here!

Those thoughts did not hang around for very long. We started to lose more games than we won. Karl Lacey was spat upon in Omagh by a supporter. Paddy McBrearty was bitten by a Dublin footballer.

Welcome to the life of being All-Ireland champs!

Our first game in the National League was against Kildare in Croke Park, on a Saturday evening double bill. We lost 2-14 to 1-13.

Our first home game since winning the All-Ireland attracted a bumper crowd, and we responded. We beat Down by five points, and Ryan McHugh made his debut, and quickly showed everyone in the ground that he was going to be an immediate added bonus to the team.

In Ballybofey, we also produced the goods against Kerry and their new manager, Eamon Fitzmaurice who was experiencing a troubled start. We had nine points to spare. But, there was no doubt about it, we found the league to be a chore. It showed in most of our performances and in our final game we hosted Dublin knowing that another defeat would see us dropping down to Division Two.

Winning would have put the lid on a spring which had been a pain in the backside, and winning would have saved us the indignity of going down. We badly wanted to win the game, and set sail towards the championship with a stronger sense of our worth as... All-Ireland champions!

We were in front for all but three minutes of the game. But when the reserve referee Michael Duffy – Padraig Hughes had to retire injured – blew his final whistle the game was level. And we were doomed.

McGuinness was as disappointed as I had seen him in such a long time. He was unhappy with the draw, and he was also not too pleased by some of the things that happened out on the field. That included a foul on me after I got on the end of Martin O'Reilly's great run through the middle 10 minutes from the finish. It should have been a penalty, and that would have sealed it for us. We would have been four up.

Instead, injury time points from Jack McCaffrey and Paul Mannion snatched away our victory. Colm had scored our goal in the 10th minute. We led 1-6 to 0-6 at half time. We were always in control, but typically of us, we lived too close to the fire. We were down.

McGuinness announced after the game to the assembled journalists that, basically, he did not give a rat's ass about being relegated.

But, privately, he was not the happiest man. And he was doubly unhappy because Paddy had been bitten by one of the Dublin boys. After the game, the Donegal County Board officially complained to the referee. It was an episode that rattled on in the newspapers, and also in the corridors of Croke Park, for a few weeks, but in the end Paddy did not want to have to attend a hearing to give voice to the complaint.

McGuinness did not believe Paddy needed to attend either. All of the evidence, photographic, and personal testimonials from Paddy and our medical personnel, were forwarded to the hearing committee. At half time in the game we had seen the bite marks on Paddy. They were as clear as day. The GAA powers-that-be just needed to take some action, but refused to do so without Paddy's personal attendance.

It was the final nail in the coffin of our league campaign. The weeks were quickly counting down to May 26 when we were due to commence our All-Ireland title defence against Tyrone.

Back at the base of the giant mountain.

'You're moving forward...

'Or... you're moving back!

'You are never stationary.'

That was Jim McGuinness' firm belief. That is what he always warned us. In March and April of 2013, I was definitely moving backwards.

And I was not the only one on the Donegal squad!

In Brian McEniff's second year of his fifth term as manager, back in 2004, he and I had still struggled to get on the same wavelength.

That fault was more mine than his, obviously.

I had started my post-graduate studies in St Pat's in Drumcondra in Dublin. The Donegal football team did not govern my life. Little things left me disjointed, like the time Brian told me I would be starting against Antrim in the championship. Brian Roper was struggling with an injury. On the Tuesday evening, Brian told me I was starting.

On the Thursday evening, he told me I was back on the substitutes bench. I was raging. I was ringing Brendan Devenney and telling him I was quitting. 'This man doesn't like me!' I told him.

'Hang about... hang about!'

Brendan told me to be patient.

We beat Antrim by six points, and Tyrone by four in the Ulster championship. There was no game time for me. In the Ulster final we got thumped by Armagh, 3-15 to 0-11. The following week Eamon McGee and Brian McLaughlin were chucked off the panel for disciplinary reasons. Same old... same old!

The summer of 2004 would belong to Fermanagh as much as anybody else, and they had a thrilling run to the All-Ireland semi-final and were cruelly denied a place in the All-Ireland final after losing out on a replay to Mayo. Fermanagh had beaten us in the Qualifiers by one point.

I was living the life of a student. I did not train as I should have when I was in college in Dublin. I was not one hundred per cent committed. I was not doing all of the things that I now know I needed to be doing.

But, I had an inkling back then as well that I was not giving it my all. Besides, I was a Donegal footballer. I was part of a Donegal team that always self-destructed. Everyone knew that.

I knew it.

Donegal were always sure to press the implode button. It was only a matter of which week in high summer?

Two weeks before the start of the 2005 championship, I knew McEniff did not have me in his plans for Armagh. We would draw with them in the quarter final, 0-12 each, and they would beat us by seven points in the replay six days later, 3-11 to 1-10. We finished the game with 12 players. McEniff also lost it on the sideline, which was unusual to see him going irate. Eamon Roper and Eamon McGee went off on two yellows, Adrian Sweeney got a straight red. Before all of that, I made a personal statement about what I thought of our hopes in the championship.

I did so silently, but I made it all the same by skipping off to Liverpool for a few days and telling McEniff that I still had some exams to do and could not get to training.

Liverpool were playing in the Champions League final against AC Milan in the Ataturk Stadium in Istanbul, in Turkey. I did not have the money to get out there, but I did wish to be part of the historic game. So, a group of us hightailed it on the boat to the home of The Beatles, Kevin Keegan, John Barnes, and Jamie Carraher and Steven Gerrard. The championship was just around the corner.

I didn't care.

My exams had already finished in St Pat's, but I didn't want McEniff to know that. Or that I was heading for the boat with Damien McClafferty, Michael Harte, Stephen Fowley, John Paul Clarke, David O'Herlihy, Dave Curtin and a big group of other mates. We situated ourselves in John Aldridge's bar.

Aldo's Bar was hopping.

The game was still hours away, but it was mad in there. It was crazier still, for all of the wrong reasons, when Liverpool found themselves 3-0 down at half time. Paolo Maldini got Milan's first, Hernan Crespo the two after that. A pin could not drop in the place without causing a stir, and then an Evertonian raced into the pub and lifted up his shirt and roared... 'Come on... THE TOFFEES!' He turned and quickly scampered out. The evening looked a total disaster.

Gerrard scored to give us some hope. Then, in six amazing minutes, Vladimir Smicer and Xabi Alonso got two more. The bar went berserk when Liverpool won the penalty shoot-out.

Liverpool were champions of Europe.

The decision was made in the early hours of the morning to stay in the city another 24 hours. We wanted to be there for the team's homecoming the following evening. And what a sight it was!

On Friday morning, in the early hours, we all got the boat back to Dublin. After Armagh, Donegal beat Wicklow in round one of the Qualifiers. In round two we lost to Cavan by a point. Wasn't I the smart boy to spend time in Liverpool?

Or was I?

In the huddle, out on the pitch after drawing with Dublin, McGuinness had reminded us that we were a championship team.

A team aimed at the big time.

We did a five-day camp back in Johnstown House Hotel as we prepared for Tyrone. No stone was left unturned. In addition, we had Karlo back, or we thought we had him back! His whole summer would be interrupted. He had played absolutely no football since the All-Ireland final, as he nursed his long standing hip injury which finally needed surgery. He had been crowned Footballer of the Year at the end of 2012.

He was 28 years-old and had four Allstar awards to his name, but he was starting from the bottom in 2013 just like the rest of us.

McGuinness was unable to name the team that started the All-Ireland final. Karlo and Mark McHugh had late setbacks in training, and Declan and David Walsh stepped up. Though Karlo and McHugh would come into the game.

I had prepared for Sean Cavanagh in the middle of the field. Instead, I found Joe McMahon there. Cavanagh went inside, where Eamon McGee picked him up. I spent the rest of the afternoon with McMahon, until Joe was sent off after receiving a second yellow card 10 minutes from the end.

Twelve months earlier, they had stayed with our high tempo on the field for about three-quarters of the game, before we got the upper hand. Since then, they had beaten us in the league in Omagh, and they had found a new keeper, Niall Morgan who was quite deadly in picking out men with his kicks and was also aping Stephen Cluxton and coming up the field to assume free kick taking duties. Tyrone looked stronger.

Ballybofey was a 17,500 sell-out for several weeks.

The game turned on Ross Wherity's goal.

Tyrone had worked doubly hard in the second quarter to fight back from a three points deficit and sneak one point in front. Myself and Big Neil were not doing great in the middle. It was wet and muggy, and they started to get a lot of the breaks before half time.

But we sucker-punched them just before the break. Murph was fouled in the middle of the field. Paddy got under a high ball, heard Colm give him a shout and flicked it down, and McFadden, although the angle was tight, hit an immaculate strike for a goal which left us 1-6 to 0-7 in front at half time.

That was the 'Too Good' moment for Donegal. The 'Too Bad' moment for Tyrone was when Stephen O'Neill attempted to go shoulder to shoulder with Neil McGee as he was breaking out from the back with the ball. O'Neill bounced off him and landed on his backside. The home crowd cheered with delight.

Ross is a St Eunan's man, and one of those laid back types. But he had been one of the few boys who had a good league campaign and he started popping up at crucial times and taking important scores for us. He can pop up unnoticed. He's a drifter on the field, but he's also good in the air, and a good option for kick outs. When he came in early enough in the second half there were four of us across the middle, myself and Ross, Big Neil and Martin McElhinney and we were winning a lot more ball.

We would end up beating Tyrone by a bigger margin than in 2012. The victory left them at a low point after such a decent performance, and it left us targetting a three in a row of Ulster titles. History was in our hands.

Justin McNulty and Sean Cavanagh scored a quick pair of points to level the game shortly after the interval, and the game had looked on the line for a short period of time. Papa then took one of those disguised kick outs of his!

He found me out on the wing. Justin McMahon fouled me, but I managed to get back up on my feet quickly enough and took a fast free that found Paddy. McBrearty turned his man, skinned Dermot Carlin completely down the right hand side of the field, and palmed the ball across the goalmouth.

Ross had floated into space.

He was only on the field a matter of seconds, but he palmed the ball to the net. It was 2-6 to 0-9, which was not the most flattering scoreline in the world, but it left us sitting strong and dominant to see out the final quarter. We kicked the next four points. Tyrone went scoreless for 32 minutes.

2-10 to 0-10 was a message, as well as a victory.

It looked as though McGuinness had been as good as his word when he had dismissed the league. We had produced it on the bigger day.

It meant a lot to be able to lay down the law in front of a team like Tyrone, no doubt about that. For several years, Harte had been watching his boys do that when it really mattered.

So, it was good that we could stand up when it counted. While there was no love lost between us and Tyrone, we all admired them. We'd be stupid if we did not! As a spectator in Croke Park, sitting at All-Ireland finals, I had willed them to win, especially in 2008.

Now, we had replaced them.

But, I wondered how strong we were actually standing our ground as so many other good teams circled us?

In my mind, I was telling myself that we were alright, but looking back at it now I know that we were not in the same place as we had been in 2012. We had not got the same 'hard yards' behind us. We had a big championship victory, yes, but the stamina work? The strength and conditioning? In truth, it had not been done as well as 2012.

We had not pushed ourselves half as hard. I had no idea, as we enjoyed the evening of our win over Tyrone, that we would pay a price for that; that as the championship stretched itself out through the middle of the summer, bodies would start to break down.

We were not as strong. I was not in the prime condition I had been 12 months before. Neither were others, and this would all come home to roost once we got to Croke Park.

CHAPTER

Our dressing room was in a state of stress.

It was the first time I had seen it like that since Jim McGuinness' arrival. There was concern on nearly everyone's face. We all sensed that we were in some trouble, and that the second half of the Ulster final was going to take something extraordinary from us, if the game was to be turned around. Before McGuinness came in to talk to us, there were a lot of heads down.

Mark McHugh was still being treated on one of the tables in the room. I'd caught a glimpse of him as I came in.

We did not know at that stage that he had burst his ear drum, or that he would have to spend two nights in hospital. We had just seen him lifted off the field after being on the receiving end of a serious bang from Stephen Gollogly. He was out of it.

We were trailing Monaghan by four points at that stage. The game was barely 10 minutes old, and they had a 0-4 to 0-0 lead. By half-time it was 0-5 to 0-2. We didn't get our first score of the Ulster final until the 32nd minute. That was a free from Colm. In injury time, Frank McGlynn stormed up to get our second point. We were shaken.

We were shocked by that first half.

When the game was finally over, Eamon McGee told me he was never going to wear white boots again.

It was the first time he had ever worn white boots. He was deadly serious.

He went home and gave them to a club mate of his, who played for Gaoth Dobhair reserves. He was disgusted by our performance, and by those new boots of his.

But, coming into the Ulster final in Clones, in our heads I've got to admit that most of us were guilty of wearing white boots.

We had got past Tyrone, but the injuries to the likes of Karlo were not going away. Big Neil too was struggling. And when we had finished with Down in the Ulster semi final, we had an even longer injury list. We lost Ryan Bradley and Frank McGlynn to concussions.

Down had been the last team to beat us in the Ulster championship, back in 2010. Since then we had won nine championship games in the province, and that included beating Down by 13 points in the 2012 Ulster final. But James McCartan was better prepared for us 12 months later.

We made it through with difficulty. I kicked a point and was happy to get out of there with a narrow victory. We were looking at three Ulster titles on the trot. A brilliant piece of history, perhaps, though we knew Monaghan would be ready for us in the final.

Monaghan, traditionally, were the one Ulster team outside of the 'big two' who had always given us an extra amount of bother. We had not beaten them in the championship since 1983. And they had back to back Qualifier wins over us in 2007 and 2008.

While we were aiming for three titles in quick succession, they had not claimed Ulster in 25 years. But they were in great hands in Malachy O'Rourke. He was smart and astute, and the Monaghan team boss was also a fast learner. At the same time, we believed we had too many good footballers for them.

Even with our problems.

Karlo, Mark, Frank, David Walsh, Anthony Thompson and Big Neil had all missed big chunks of games through injuries of different sorts.

Bodies were breaking up.

And the bodies in yellow shirts out on the field were slow, and lethargic, from the first minute of the 2013 Ulster final. We were completely flat.

There was a total lack of intensity. Instead, we were on the receiving end. We were giving nothing back. We had tried to come out and play a more open game, but O'Rourke had exploited that, and had ordered his men to send long direct balls into his full forward line.

It was my man, Darren Hughes who opened the scoring for them. Then they shot over frees from their keeper, Rory Beggan and Conor McManus. Eight minutes in, Padraig Donaghy whacked one over from far out to make it 0-4 to 0-0. It was a furious eight minutes.

After that, McHugh got whacked in a tackle.

We were running down alleyways. Drew Wylie was stopping Colm from getting any ball. Colin Walshe was out in front of Paddy. Murph was losing his battle with Vinny Corey. And that's how it would stay to the bitter end. Our full forward line did not get one score from play.

But the blame wasn't solely theirs! At the other end of the field Kieran Hughes was giving Eamon McGee a torrid time. His brother, Darren was laying down the law in the middle third of the field, and I was not able to do anything about it. There was not one man in our dressing room at half time who felt that he had showed up for the Ulster final.

In the first 10 minutes of the second half, Kieran Hughes kicked three points that effectively buried us.

Back home in the Mount Errigal Hotel in Letterkenny, McGuinness said that the management team were to blame for the result. He said they got it wrong, that they had left Murph inside in the full forward line for too long. In fact, the Ulster final of 2013 put an end to Murph ever again playing as an out and out full forward.

As players, we had let our standards slip throughout the year and we were left with a six day turnaround before meeting Laois in round four of the Qualifiers in Carrick-on-Shannon.

Darren Hughes had beaten me for the 70 minutes.

There was no doubt about that in my mind. The game left me convinced that I was struggling for form, and I went down to Carrick-on-Shannon with too many doubts cluttering up my brain. I was off form, I did not feel strong. I knew that, but what I did not know was that my struggles with Hughes would continue over the next 12 months and that, as a result, McGuinness would also begin to lose faith in me.

I did not feel that I was ready at all for Laois. It was the first time we would ever play them in the championship. And we would do so without McHugh sweeping so brilliantly through our defence. We would also find Laois in a mood to try to physically bully us.

We beat them, in the end, 0-14 to 0-8. There's a photo of a Laois supporter outside the ground appearing to take a piss on my newly sponsored car. Colm Parkinson tweeted the photograph and it was spoken about on *Off the Ball* on Newstalk. I played football with 'Wolly' in Maynooth. He was always good craic and little did I know it then, I'd be a guest on the show just a few weeks later after our horror show against Mayo! My name was on the side of the luminous green car along with the Donegal crest. It was given to me by Divers garage in Letterkenny and my wife had driven it to the game. I should've told her to leave it at home. It stood out. You could have seen it from the moon.

It seemed to me that most of the country had been wanting to piss on Donegal's parade for most of 2013. McGuinness, afterwards, and in the days following, the whole way to our All-Ireland quarter final meeting with Mayo, was livid.

He felt that we were on the receiving end of extra punishment as reigning All-Ireland champions, but that we were not getting the protection, or fairness, from referees.

McGuinness was not delighted with me either.

He was getting on my case more and more in the dressing room. He wanted to know why I was not bossing people like I had been doing in 2012? He told me I had to step it back up.

But, I did not feel I was ready for Croke Park, and everything that awaited us in the final stretch of our All-Ireland title defence. Psychologically I was in a poor place. Every footballer knows in his heart when he is not quite there! Was I being a ruthless f***** in 2013? Did I prepare like one?

No, I got distracted like everybody else.

I knew I was struggling to make contact with my opponent when he came at us, and putting the press on in two zones was suddenly twice as hard for me. I was searching for excuses, rather than choosing to work my way out of my difficulties.

Why was I not bringing authority into the game?

All through 2012 I had done that, and loved bringing it, and the bigger and more difficult the opponent, the more I relished doing it.

In 2012, I had been the man initiating the physical stuff.

Why am I not looking for that?

Why do I not want it?

Questions and excuses were littering my head. Instead of setting the agenda with my opponent, I was letting myself get pushed and dragged. And I was accepting this.

I was not putting up any sort of fight.

What's wrong here?

McGuinness was such an expert judge on the training field.

At the end of each session, he liked to get us to do four or five 200 metre sprints, starting on the 45 metres line, around the goalposts, and back up to the opposite 45 metres line.

Each of those sprints is a hard run.

McGuinness could see in my body language that I was not myself. I knew he could see it, like he could almost see through me.

At half time in games, he was having a go.

And it would be the same in 2014. He thought I was playing in my comfort zone. And my performances backed up that assumption.

St Eunan's were after clinching our three in a row of county titles, when John Joe Doherty asked me to be his team captain.

John Joe was the new Donegal manager, taking over from Brian McIver, and beating Jim McGuinness to the top job. It was a massive honour, but I also knew what John Joe wanted from me. He saw me as one of the new breed of Donegal footballers, who could put our problems and failures of old to one side, and crack on into the future.

I had not expected the question.

We talked about my role for the year, and I thanked him. He told me I was the standout candidate for the captaincy because of my consistent performances. He wanted me to lead by example on the field.

I quickly grew into the role.

I became captain, and from that year on I remained one of the team leaders. And I never looked back from that point, not until 2013.

Until 2013, I had brought authority to everything I did in training, and especially into games. Although being awarded the captaincy in 2009 was very much the making of me as a Donegal footballer, it was also at times almost the breaking of me as well.

The messing and the shit went on all year from start to finish. There was always someone acting the idiot who had to be sorted out. I never had to deal with all of the messing before, but in 2009, suddenly, everything seemed to be going through me.

I had to offer my advice.

It was all new to me. I had known in Donegal, down through the years, that there had never been a dull moment, but I had absolutely no idea what it was like to have to handle all of those same moments.

All the same, that year was the making of me. I stepped up as a man, beginning when we won the McKenna Cup at the start of the year. We played Queens in the final. Under new experimental rules that were being trialled, anyone who picked up a booking had to be substituted. So, after receiving a yellow card during the game I left the field and was replaced. Later, as captain, when I went up to accept the cup I was stopped in my tracks by Danny Murphy, the Ulster Council secretary.

'Sorry Rory... you can't go up and accept the cup!'

'What?' I replied.

'You can't accept the cup!'

'What...?

'WHY?'

Murphy told me I was suspended, which, I found out later, was not technically the case.

I thought it was a joke.

It was one of those horrible winter nights. Conall Dunne was wrapped in foil after the game, it was so damned cold.

I turned around. Barry Monaghan went up and accepted the cup instead. After that, I vowed never to back down as a Donegal footballer again.

Going down to Croke Park as Ulster champions is something special. We only realised that in August of 2013, when we headed to Dublin for our All-Ireland quarter final against Mayo.

It felt different.

We were the same team that had gone down to Croker in 2011 and 2012, but we were not reigning champs. We had not proven ourselves No.1 in Ulster. The back door was... the back door!

At the same time, Mayo were mentally weak as far as we were concerned. We knew they were a team that cracked under pressure. All we had to do was to apply it. Like the 2012 All-Ireland final.

Simple.

My job was to pick up Donal Vaughan. He was one of their defenders who liked to break forward at every opportunity. Horan liked to see Vaughan on a charge. In the 14th minute of the game he took off.

Mark McHugh and myself were exchanging passes. I passed the ball off to him, and ran ahead. But Mark slipped.

They intercepted the ball.

In fairness, they just took off with it. They broke so quickly. From the opening minute, with Keith Higgins playing around the middle of the field and racing into attack, there was a whole different zip to their game. When Vaughan took off, there was no way I was getting back to do anything about him. He was gone.

I was 40 metres behind him.

Vaughan ended up rounding Papa and slipping the ball into the net for their second goal. Cillian O'Connor had scored their first to put them 1-2 to 0-0 in front after six minutes.

We got three points on the bounce, and tried to steady the game. After that, we wanted to impose our terms on the game, same as usual, same as we had done against them the year before. But when Vaughan scored they were 2-3 to 0-4 in front at the end of the first quarter.

It went from bad to worse.

Lee Keegan, Colm Boyle, the whole lot of them were bombing forward. Aidan O'Shea was catching so much ball in the middle, and every time he did so he horsed through our tackles.

Higgins continued to be dynamic.

They got better and better. One mistake was leading directly to another mistake, as McGuinness had always warned us they would.

'One man makes a mistake... the next man will probably make one too!' He was certain in that message.

And we made enough mistakes to allow them to reach an unbelievable score of 4-17. We had thrown in the towel long before the finish.

That's how they got to that total.

We had quit.

'Are the legs gone, Rory?' I was asked immediately afterwards, before we'd even left Croke Park, by BBC Radio Foyle journalist Enda McClafferty – my bloody next door neighbour.

With a wry smile, I replied, 'We'll have to wait and see. I'm not going to make any hasty decisions.'

Behind the smile, I was unsure.

We allowed 13 different Mayo footballers to get on the scoresheet. We resigned ourselves to the heaviest defeat ever suffered by reigning All-Ireland champions since Dublin had surrendered their title to Kerry in 1978 and shipped five goals, three of them coming from the Bomber Liston.

That day it was 5-11 to 0-9.

Our 4-17 to 1-10 defeat was a complete systems failure. In the previous 17 championship games under Jim McGuinness we had conceded a total of four goals only. But in 47 minutes against Mayo we had coughed up the exact same number.

It was embarrassing. Not just for us, but for our families and our friends sitting in the ground watching us being humiliated. Of course, reaching such a low would become the supreme catalyst for bouncing back in 2014, and when the time came to talk about 2014 the rawness of losing to Mayo by 16 points was still very much there.

As we drowned our sorrows, a few of the lads dubbed it... 'The Rory Kavanagh and Eamon McGee Retirement Party'.

We decided to go somewhere quiet, so we headed for Downings. It was where it started for us all under McGuinness, and in August 2013 it seemed like the place it would end as well.

I'd been substituted against Mayo and Eamon was sent off. We'd not even said much about possible retirement but at the same time, we fuelled the fire.

'We're gone,' we'd both say... '... gone!'

And we were soon gone. Kathryn arrived in Downings to pick us up. She was double-jobbing; she was told by Eamon's girlfriend to get him home as well.

We had poor Kathryn tortured the whole way home. We were soon plonked at my kitchen table, eating crisps and talking shite.

Kathryn popped her head in the door. As she turned for the living room, she said, 'aren't you two boys glad you're home?'

Eamon shook his head, looking at me in disgust.

'Eamon McGee doesn't take orders from anyone,' he then said, for some reason now speaking in the third person.

Our discussion, getting increasingly serious now – no shite talk – turned to how could we get out again? The evening was still young.

After all, it was OUR retirement party. We'd our ups and downs in our careers but sitting at my kitchen table eating Hunky Dorys buffalo flavoured crisps on a Monday night would've been a sad way to go out.

We needed a plan.

With no key for the back door and with Kathryn watching television in the other room, our main avenue of escape out the front door was blocked.

'I'm outta here,' Eamon said, as he walked towards the kitchen window.

'Headed for the town.'

I turned to watch a 6 feet 2 inches, 14-and-a-half stone man try to manoeuvre his way out my kitchen window. But he did, and off he went into the darkness. I sat there for a minute or two, thinking.

I sized up the window.

I'd a bit more difficulty than Eamon but was making commendable progress. I'd swung a leg out the window.

Now, I was half-in and half-out. Just as I was about to lift the other leg, the kitchen door opened. It was Kathryn.

And she just stared at me.

I stared back at her.

We didn't say anything for a minute. We just continued to stare at one another. And stare some more.

I had a look on my face, like the little boy who has just got caught with his hand in the biscuit jar.

'What the hell are you doing?' she demanded.

I was still staring.

'Eamon's away out the window,' I replied.

'I better go get him.'

I swung over my left leg and landed safely in the back garden.

I took off, still wondering how far he had gone.

I soon found him. He was out at the entrance to the estate, waiting on a taxi. We flagged one down and off we went into the night.

Nobody tells Eamon McGee what to do.

We waited a month before talking about it.

Whether we were going to retire?

The only man in the family to leave Croke Park happy that summer was my cousin Joe Boyle, who captained the Donegal hurlers to the Nicky Rackard title.

Jim McGuinness wanted to know if we really wanted to fight to win back our Ulster title? Come back to Croke Park as champions, and look to take back our All-Ireland as well? He asked Murph to take us on his own for a team meeting, and to come back to him with an answer.

Murph called us together in Donegal Town. Murph wanted to know if every single man in the room was prepared to give one hundred per cent in 2014?

I still had some doubts.

At the meeting, I realised that my commitment was wavering, and I spoke up honestly in front of Murph and the boys.

Murph said McGuinness wanted every man back hard at work from November, that we were going to do everything properly. That McGuinness wanted us to work twice as hard as before.

I sat there, listening, and I wanted to be one hundred per cent with the boys, but I found myself holding back. I had my reasons, good reasons. Kathryn was expecting our first child in January of 2014, and my No.1 commitment was to my wife for the following three months.

Football would have to come second for those three months. And I told Murph and the boys how I was thinking. I said I could not commit until the new year. I was the only one who said so.

Murph kept the momentum of the meeting going.

He said everyone was in agreement.

'When this man calls us back into training,' Murph summed up, '... we are going to be there for him...

'Apart from Rory.

'Rory can see how things go with the baby... and he'll be in contact with Jim.

'Everyone else?

'Agreed?'

We were only an hour together in the Abbey Hotel. I walked out of the room in a little bit of a daze. I knew my commitment levels dropping were the first signs of me walking away from the team. But I was not ready to walk away. Looking back on it from my retirement 12 months later, I realise I was not prepared to put in the maximum amount of hard graft that Jim McGuinness was demanding.

The boys got back into the gym

Meanwhile, I did a bit on my own. When McGuinness started the running on the beach in Dunfanaghy, he called me. It was the middle of November, and I turned up alright, but I was unable to do any of the brutal training.

After losing to Mayo, myself and Kathryn had taken a quick break in Sorento. I needed to get away from everything, and do nothing. I was lying by the side of the pool one afternoon when, suddenly, inexplicably, I got a searing pain down my right hamstring.

I was literally lying there, when it came upon me.

It came from nowhere.

I tried to swim, but every time I went to sit down on a chair I had this pain running up my back. I tried to do some running. I wanted it to pass, but when I got back to training with St Eunan's it was still there.

The pain was unrelenting.

For six weeks, I could not get rid of it. Every time I went training with the club, I found I could not sprint. I was only able to reach sixty per cent. I was totally at a loss to understand what had happened to my body?

I visited our county physio, Dermot Simpson.

I explained it to McGuinness. I was genuinely concerned about the injury, and Dermot sent me for scans, but nothing showed up. Dermot explained it was looking like hamstring tendinopothy and that it was a tricky injury to treat. He wanted me to get needle therapy.

The pain was really wrecking me, and the only way to deal with it was with needles. Needles, and more needles.

Over the course of the couple of months the pain began to slowly go. But McGuinness was watching me on the beach in Dunfanaghy. He was watching me, and I was watching on as the boys headed out into the biting cold wind and rain. And when we went to Castlefin, McGuinness was still watching me.

'Not training tonight?' he'd ask.

'No... I can't do it, Jim!'

And a week later.

'Not training... again?' he'd ask.

'No... can't!'

He knew that I was the only one who had been slow to commit at the team meeting. And he was watching me miss out on the hardest work of the whole year. The man was seriously wondering about me.

The trust between us was breaking down.

2014

CHAPTER

Through late December and into January, I was up on the treatment table with Dermot. Religiously, after every game, he needed to get those needles into me in order to ease away the pain that continued to come back through my hamstring, and speed its way up my lower back.

I was still missing some training sessions because of the ache, and McGuinness continued to question me. He would give me that look.

That look said everything.

But, he'd also occasionally pipe up.

'Are you not training again, tonight?'

'Listen Jim, this is still sore...' I'd reply.

The lack of trust began to play on my mind. He thought I was looking to take the easy road at the start of the year. I could see it written on his face. He thought I was trying to miss the hard yards.

I went to every training session in December and early January, but I'd stay in my street clothes as the boys changed into all of their gear, and got ready to battle the elements, the gale force winds, the hailstones, whatever Dunfanaghy or Castlefin decided to conjure up?

We were so lucky with the backroom team we had.

Charlie McManus was our doc and friend. But everyone was our friend. Mr Kevin Moran, the team's surgeon, Dermot Simpson our physio, and the team's physical therapists, JD McGrenra and the former county star, Donal Reid. I used to pop into Sean Reilly when I felt a bit stiff or sore. He was a great man for getting the body right. Then in the gym, we had the excellence of Eugene Eivers and Adam Speer in charge of our strength and conditioning. Adam would like his 'Speersy Specials' as he called them. They were Wednesday morning gym sessions that combined some aerobic and strength work that would test us to our core. Charlie Molloy was our masseuse, Declan Gallagher looked after video analysis and stats, while Joe McCloskey and Charles McGuinness were the kitmen.

JD was brilliant, one of those really positive people, someone who would just put you in good form every time you chatted with him. I had some great laughs with him. During the week of a big championship game he would drive all around the county getting work done with different players.

He might leave Dublin at six o'clock in the morning and drive to Glenties and get started with the Adrara and Glenties boys. Then he'd hike it over to Donegal Town to Karlo. After that, it was on to Letterkenny where he might work on three or four of us.

I would ring Terry McEniff in the Mount Errigal Hotel to make sure there was a room available for him to set up in. I might order a plate of sandwiches and a jug of Miwadi orange for him, and he would be happy with that. Then, he would have to travel over to Gaoth Dobhair to get to Neil McGee and Odhran MacNiallais. By the time he was finished it could be eight o'clock in the evening, and he had a drive back to Dublin ahead of him.

But he loved it.

He took great satisfaction in being part of the whole thing.

'Hop up on the plinth there...' he'd tell me.

'It's great, isn't it Rory? The journey we're on...'

'It's unbelievable JD....'

'Ah yeah, Rory...it's bloody great!'

Of course, there would be the odd falling out among the medical staff, usually when it came to the diagnosis of injuries. Everything had to go through Dr Charlie McManus, Mr Kevin Moran and then Dermot Simpson. There was disagreement on certain issues, and often meetings were called between the management and medical team to sort some things out.

Injuries were just a fact of life due to the intensity of our training sessions, and bodies broke down regularly. In fairness to Jim he put a great backroom team together, and each member played a huge role in our success.

Dermot was excellent at making sure we were fully recovered before returning to full training. Very methodical, he always made sure the rehab of an injury was done to the letter of the law. I spent a fair part of 2014 on Dermot's plinth getting dry needling done.

I would meet with Charlie and Kevin too. Whether it was for a blood test, flu jab or arranging a scan. They got it done. Pronto. No messing about. They made it happen so that we could recover in the quickest possible time.

Charlie and Kevin both shared a great sense of humour and we could approach them about anything. And Kevin took a fair bit of stick after our All-Ireland quarter final in Croke Park in 2014 when he was sent flying through the air by Armagh's Aaron Findon. He was nicknamed the 'flying doc' by a good few of us for the rest of the year, but he took it well.

It was an unnecessary act by Findon and Kevin could've made a big deal about it. He was getting calls from local and national media to do interviews but he declined each time. He told me that he got a call from Findan apologising for what he'd done, and Kevin was happy to leave it at that.

I had my fair share of injuries during McGuinness' four years but I only missed two championship games due to injury, once against Derry in 2012 and once against Antrim in 2014.

That's testament to the work of the medical team.

Discipline was something absolutely sacred to McGuinness. Losing our heads was considered unforgivable.

I was already in a bad place in my relationship with him at the start of 2014 after my failure, in his eyes, to match everyone else in the hard grinding work in November and December, on the dunes in Dunfanaghy, and out on the wind battered field in Castlefin.

When my discipline caved in a few months into the year, I was doubly in trouble with McGuinness. On the morning of the 2014 Ulster final, as we faced another fraught afternoon with Monaghan, he told me that I was out of the team. But he did not take me aside and personally break the news.

Instead, he called out the team at our final sit down that Sunday morning in the Slieve Russell Hotel. I had fully expected to play.

But McGuinness did not trust me.

Simple as that. He thought I was a liability, and he was possibly right, but that did not ease the blow.

I had worked myself back into the team for the early rounds of the league, and had put in some good performances. We were making a whole fresh start. McGuinness had dispensed with Rory and Maxi and Francie Friel, and brought in his new management team. He was now in conclave with Damien Diver, John Duffy and Paul McGonigle.

We were down in Division Two, but we were flying in many ways. We had Armagh, Down, Galway, Laois, Louth, Meath and Monaghan for company, which was high grade opposition. We got stuck into it.

We went down to Portlaoise and beat Laois by 13 points to begin with, 2-19 to 1-9, rattling up an impressive score. We then travelled down to Galway and came home with another convincing win. Next up, we had Monaghan on my home turf in O'Donnell Park, Letterkenny.

I was looking forward to that one all week long. I had revenge on my mind. But Darren Hughes did not start for Monaghan, and some of the goodness of our 2-11 to 0-10 victory was sucked out of the game for me. Though I was playing well, and starting every game.

My only problem was that I wasn't lasting the full 70 minutes. I was being called ashore early in the second half in most league games. This was partly due to my injury, but Jim also felt that I wasn't fit enough to last the full game. I knew in advance of most games that I'd be coming off. It was something that Jim talked about. He took me off after 48 minutes against Laois, and after 40 minutes against Monaghan, straight after half time. He was taking a bit of stick in the local media after that. But Jim did not think I had 70 minutes in me, and I could not convince him he was wrong. We lost to Down, but by early April we were exactly where we wanted to be.

We were beating Armagh in our final divisional game, ensuring promotion to Division One, and sending them through the trapdoor to Division Three, which was a surprise since Kieran McGeeney had joined Paul Grimley on the sideline. It was my best performance of the year. I scored three points and set up Murph for our second goal in our 2-10 to 1-8 win, but I was still called ashore before the end.

I was happy with my club form. In mid-April, St Eunan's travelled the four miles to take on a Glenswilly side who had won the county championship the previous October before making it the whole way to the Ulster club final, where they would lose to a good Ballinderry Shamrocks side.

From our point of view, 2013 had ended up on a sour note for the club. We'd been firm favourites to defeat a developing Malin side in the quarter finals only to fall flat on our faces and lose, 3-12 to 1-7.

We needed to lay down a marker in 2014 and, even though it was just a league match, winning was important.

Big Neil and I were in direction competition. Down the years, some days have gone for me, and other days for him, but I left Glenswilly content that afternoon following a 3-13 to 1-7 St Eunan's win. I was coming into form, I felt, at the right time and hoped McGuinness would agree.

And when the county final came around later that year, I was captain of St Eunan's against Neil and Murph's Glenswilly under the lights at MacCumhaill Park.

It was a compressed championship, with fixtures every weekend. With that, there was no real build up but the Dr Maguire was up for grabs against our neighbours and rivals.

Kevin Rafferty, my midfield partner, was forced off after only nine minutes with a serious eye injury. John Haran, at 37 and playing in his 12th county final, moved in alongside me and would later receive the 'Man of the Match' award.

We won 0-9 to 0-6.

Six months before this, Jim was telling me that I was almost fit enough to last the full game. But he seemed happy with me, nevertheless. Our difficulties at the start of the year appeared to be fading out of sight.

I was happy. We were also a happy team again, and for the first and only time in his four years, Jim had organised a warm weather training camp for us in Portugal, on the Algarve, the week after we defeated Armagh, and the week before we met Monaghan in the Division Two final in Croke Park. He told us he wanted 2014 to be the best year imaginable for each of us in terms of our preparation.

Everything looked so exactly right.

McGuinness, in addition to having us back winning games, had received a guarantee that there would be no distractions with club championship games until Donegal finally exited the All-Ireland series.

We had no excuses.

The spring and summer of 2009 was just one long catalogue of disciplinary issues, man after man after man. It was like there was some damned virus at work in the dressing room. Everybody had half a mind to go AWOL.

The problems and the bureaucracy was dragging me down like quick sand. I was working like a madman trying to motivate the team, talk to boys who were acting like fools, trying to get my own game together, and I was not prepared for any of it. It was burning me out.

Worst of all, amongst the boys on the mess at some stage in 2009 was Big Neil, the man who had a strong word in my ear when he was captain in 2007 and I was acting like an idiot.

Big Neil in June of that year was shown the door.

That killed me. Big Neil, back then, was such an important player, but Doherty's word was strong and he refused to back down. And I had to live with my manager's decision.

Antrim came to Ballybofey in the first round of the championship and did a number on us by a single point, 1-10 to 0-12. We kicked something like 20 wides.

I spent half an hour talking to the media after the game, and I had to put on my strongest, most positive face and try to make sense of what was happening and protect the team. That was a trick! I talked about regrouping and coming good in the middle of the summer, and I did not believe a word coming out of my own mouth. But we were lucky to get Carlow in the Qualifiers, then Clare.

In the third round of the Qualifiers we had a gigantic 2-13 to 0-18 victory over Derry after extra time. The two easy games had helped us recover after the speed bump that was Antrim. Beating Derry on a Saturday night in front of an electric crowd in Ballybofey was the tonic our year needed. Again I had played well and thought to myself this could be a turning point.

It was a furious contest. We shared 10 wides between us in the first few minutes, but Murph, who gave an exhibition of football against the brilliant Sean Marty Lockhart, and Cass eased us into the lead and we were stubborn enough, and somehow strong-willed that evening. Coming off the field that evening, I felt that the Donegal team I was leading were ready and able for anybody. We beat Galway by a point in Sligo, and put the head down for Cork in the All-Ireland quarter final. They uppercutted us.

1-27 to 2-10.

Another long journey home from Dublin for those who wished to get onto the team bus.

I was devastated, and totally deflated.

In addition, I was physically drained.

The whole year left me with nothing left. I was a long slim bottle of someone's favourite drink. I was empty. And I had to have a word with John Joe and advise him that I was going to forget all about football for as long as possible. I told him I was going away for three months, maybe four or five months.

I was not sure.

But, I knew for certain that I needed a long break after the toughest year of my life as a Donegal footballer.

McGuinness said more than once that he wanted 2014 to be the best year of our lives. No stone was going to be left unturned, no obstacle not removed with some force.

At an early season team meeting in the Station House Hotel in Letterkenny, before we queued up as usual and signed the sheet of paper which promised our fullest commitment for the rest of the year, he had flipped up his chart in front of us. There was one figure on the white sheet. It was staring back at us all.

361 DAYS.

'What's that?' asked Jim.

What is it, we asked ourselves.

There were a few idle suggestions. The number of training sessions we did in 2013? The number we're going to do in 2014?

'That is the number of days until the All-Ireland final!' Jim announced triumphantly.

'That may seem like a long way off to you now boys!

'But it's not,' he continued. 'It's just under 12 months.

'Those months will become weeks... and the weeks will become days...

'And then... we' ll be in the All-Ireland final.'

It was powerful stuff to watch.

Even more so the evening before the 2014 All-Ireland final when the flipchart reappeared at the top of the meeting room in the Johnstown House Hotel. Jim pulled up the first page.

Just one number was presented.

1 DAY.

'Now... WE'RE HERE!' he said.

One week of warm weather training was of more value than any of us had imagined. It was the paradise of being a professional sportsman for almost seven days.

We trained morning and afternoon.

We also did more kicking of the ball than we had ever done. McGuinness had a rectangle on the field every single day. He wanted a pattern of play burned into our brains by the end of the week. One man gave a dink pass to the next man up the short side of the rectangle. The next man put his boot through the ball and sent it diagonally across the rectangle.

This was repeated. For hours and hours, all week long. It was so simple, but simplicity in games is often the most difficult of items to locate.

Dink... diagonal.

Dink... diagonal.

The heat was energising. Our gym sessions were invigorating. A recovery in the pool was followed by some light stretching. There was a short nap after lunch, of course. And to the next day.

Dink... diagonal.

Dink... diagonal.

We did everything we wanted to do, and we did not mention Monaghan and the impending Division Two league final once.

In the 39th minute of the league final, or shortly after as I reached the sideline and got a glancing look from McGuinness that threatened to cut me into two, my last year as a Donegal footballer went into a tailspin once again. Except this time it was much worse than it had looked at the beginning of the year.

David Gough, the Meath referee, had sent me to the line. I was in a state of shock. I could not believe what I had just done, and afterwards McGuinness did not shy away from telling the media that what I had done was completely and totally unacceptable in his book.

He did not spare me.

Though, I knew in my heart I did not deserve to be spared. But, it had all happened so quickly. I could not believe, as I walked off the field, what I had done?

I had been chasing back into defence after a Monaghan player. And, somehow, my boot had got tangled up and came off my foot. I continued running into defence with one bare foot. The ball went wide.

I came jogging back out to the middle of the field to go and find my boot, to discover two Monaghan boys playing with it. They were tossing it over and back to one another. Darren Hughes had it in his hand.

'Are you going to give me my boot?' I said to Hughes.

He gave me back an earful.

No boot.

I looked over to the linesman, and shouted at him. Meanwhile, my boot was still in the air.

'You don't need it anyway...' Hughes yelled, '... the way you're playing!'

Then he threw my boot away in the distance. I went and took my boot up and started to undo the laces. Hughes was standing over me as I did so, standing far too close.

Hughes was giving me more jip.

'You're right...' I told him.

'You have us beat here... course you do!' I continued.

I was happy to be laughing back at him for those few seconds, but then a firework went off in my brain.

F*** you...!

And I poked him in the general vicinity of his balls with my boot which was still in my hand, and not on my foot.

The linesman was sprinting towards me, and had seen everything.

I was given a straight red card.

It was just as we were coming back into the game, and the cold stare from McGuinness informed me that I had let him and all of the boys down badly. There was no handshake, no word of sympathy.

I knew he was disgusted.

And I know that moment of madness from me, and that look from him, was what cost me my starting place in the Ulster final two months later when we got back face to face with Monaghan in Clones.

McGuinness had two negatives against my name. My reluctance, in his mind, to do the hard yards. And my indiscipline. In the lead up to the Ulster final I was doing a lot of talking at team meetings about meeting the physical challenge of Monaghan head on.

I was saying, too often in the weeks leading into the game, that we needed to put down some serious markers with these boys.

McGuinness did not like what he was hearing from me.

I think he saw me as a ticking bomb

He saw me wanting revenge on Darren Hughes, and he feared my emotion would melt over a second time. He never said anything to me, however.

At one team meeting he played a DVD of Monaghan, and during it he asked Murph to take charge of the flipchart and to tick boxes analysing

Monaghan's use of the ball. The meeting was deep into discussing Monaghan in detail, and McGuinness and Murph were painting a picture of how they wanted to play and how they would look to work us, in particular their long delivery of ball inside to Conor McManus and Kieran Hughes in their full forward line.

I remember it being a long, thorough breakdown of Monaghan's style of play. As soon as there was a break in the discussion, I had piped up about our aggression levels, and laying down markers, blah, blah, blah... all of the pumped up stuff McGuinness did not want to hear at that same meeting.

I was on a different wavelength.

McGuinness knew it.

All I could see in front of me, really, was Darren Hughes. He was similar to me in lots of ways. He was athletic, and a forceful runner. He liked to play a long, driven ball inside, and he could kick his own score. He was confident in that. He had kicked one long screaming point against us in the league final, and he would kick another in the Ulster final in 2014.

Hughes was a good opponent. He liked to smash the ball down from kick outs, as I liked to do, and he was also good at the verbals. He liked them more than me, in truth.

I would laugh that talk off.

I'd heard it all before.

I just preferred to tell my man, 'You're right... you're right, you're right!' And let him talk to himself if he wanted to do so!

I saw the Ulster final as my chance to sort him out. He had beaten me twice, in the 2013 Ulster final, and also in the league final until I got dismissed.

Then, I was stopped in my tracks.

My world froze over.

McGuinness called out the Ulster final team at our meeting before we left the Slieve Russell Hotel for Clones. I was not in.

My mind closed down.

I did not listen to a single word for the rest of the meeting.

I just sat there.

In a whole abandoned world of my own.

The week after we had lost the league final to Monaghan, Mark McHugh upped and left.

He was the fourth player to quit the squad in as many weeks. Antoin McFadden, Gary McFadden and Thomas McKinley had called it a day before Mark. Some of them hadn't been getting game time, and that included Mark, who had struggled that little bit to follow up his amazing performances in 2012 with the same again in 2013. A pelvis injury had forced him to miss the league in 2013, and the championship was the same for him as it was for the rest of us, and he never got back into his stride.

McHugh was only 23 years old. To have one of the team's best footballers, and someone who had been the heartbeat of the team at times, leave so fast was disturbing for us all.

Mark had not started the league final against Monaghan. He was clearly not very happy, and one evening in Castlefin, McGuinness had reared up on him in front of us all over a newspaper interview.

It was never nice to be on the receiving end, though I don't know whether Mark was especially ruffled by that. But I guessed, with everything else going on, and not getting his name on the team for the league final, it did not help much.

But, maybe a lot of the other boys were thinking the same thing about me, for all I knew?

CHAPTER 12

Moving from Plan A to Plan B, and doing so without hesitation, doing so sometimes cold-bloodedly, was part of Jim McGuinness' genius.

Every team we played was studying us just as hard as Jim McGuinness was studying them. Derry knew that we exploited our opponent's kick outs. And that my role, and the job of others in the middle, was to smash the ball back into their defence. Derry did not let us do that in the 2014 Ulster quarter final.

Their keeper was hitting the ball low and hard, but flighting it at just the exact height so that Fergal Doherty in particular could win the ball at pace, and catch it in front of his face, rather than over his head.

It was precision stuff.

I was watching from the sideline, serving my one match suspension after being sent off in the league final. All of their men in the middle were sprinting towards their own goals for each kick out and claiming the ball at speed. When Doherty went off injured midway through the first half, they continued to win all of their own ball.

Our boys could not get near it.

Our three points win was a victory that McGuinness pulled from his back pocket. For once, I was in a unique position to view the sharpness and excellence of his reactions to what was happening out there.

I was out, and Big Neil was unable to come into the game until early in the second half because of an ankle injury which he had trouble shaking off.

Christy Toye and Odhran MacNiallis started in the middle. Christy put in a huge shift and was taken out of it at half time, as McGuinness had warned him in advance, when we trailed by 0-4 to 0-6.

McGuinness reconfigured everything for the second half. Murph started on the edge of the square. Leo McLoone was moved from centre back to centre forward, and Martin McElhinney came into the middle. In the next seven minutes we won the game, and silenced the large Derry following in Celtic Park.

Anthony Thompson, who also amazed me with his workrate, ghosted forward and clipped a point to begin with. One minute later, Ryan McHugh took the ball from the kick out, Murph combined with Frank McGlynn, and Leo finished off the move with a smart shot to the net. Murph then added two glorious points, one of which left all of us on the sideline pinching ourselves, as he had so little room from a sideline ball.

Before Derry got their senses back and had cleared their heads, we were 1-9 to 0-9 in front. The game had been seized from them through the excellence of McGuinness' strategy, and some breathtaking finishing.

I was named to start against Antrim in the semi final.

And I was bursting to see some championship action. McGuinness had me detailed to take up Michael McCann, who was a hard worker for them, and a strong runner on the ball. I had my homework done. On the Wednesday evening before the game, I went down to pick up a ball, and... I felt something tear. Right below my groin I had done some damage doing the simplest thing in the world.

'What's wrong?' McGuinness shouted at me, as I walked towards the sideline slowly.

'I dunno...' I replied.

'I'm after doing something!'

He may not have been feeling sorry for me, but I more than made up for that myself. I was in shit form as well. I was about to sit out two games in a row.

Luckily for him, Odhran MacNiallais was grabbing the opportunity every chance he got, and he was kicking his points and doing a real good job in the middle third.

Good things happened when Odhran got the ball. Ryan McHugh's running and brilliant reading of the game was also making a huge difference, and Darach 'Jigger' O'Connor had come in and was pushing everyone else to maintain the highest of standards.

Antrim, like most teams, were able to put it up to us for 35 minutes. Then, once again as I watched on from the sideline, it seemed that Donegal simply said, 'To hell with this!' We scored 3-9 in the second half to win by 13 points. Wiped them off the field with such a dismissive manner.

We did so without Karlo, without me, and instead the young boys became men. O'Connor put in a furious hour's work, and in the 48th minute tore a hole through the Antrim defence, took a return pass from Frank and, as everyone expected him to take his point, he planted the ball in the net. MacNiallais struck four points, all from play. Dermot Molloy came off the bench and grabbed a goal and a point. So, from the bench that was named before the game began, we had totalled 2-7 alone. We had a four weeks break to the Ulster final. It was a long time to think and talk about Monaghan.

The fight to get on the field against Monaghan had begun. I knew I had everything to do. Big Neil was being hit by injuries and had come off the field after 19 minutes. Karlo needed to get one hundred per cent match fit.

Some of us needed every day of the four weeks.

I took off and did not come back for almost six months.

I did not even want to know anything about the Donegal football team for as long as possible. With my next door neighbour, Damien McClafferty and I were out of the country by November, 2009.

We did not come back until April the next year. I missed the entire league campaign in John Joe Doherty's second year. At the end of May 2010, I was named on the team that would lose 1-15 to 2-10 to Down in the Ulster quarter final, and by the end of June, in the first round of the Qualifiers, Armagh were 2-6 to 0-4 up at half time in Crossmaglen, and scored four more points in a burst immediately after.

They won 2-15 to 0-11 but the game was up long before that as Jamie Clarke had scored two goals in the first six minutes.

Towards the end, Colm McFadden was replaced by Adrian Hanlon. As Colm sat on the bench, the TV cameras caught him grinning. He would get abuse about that. But Colm was making his 100th appearance for Donegal that day and was asked to stay around for a presentation on the pitch afterwards. He didn't want to do it. Not there. Not then.

Colm was making a joke at his own expense when the cameras found him.

After being forced to stand for photographs, he was barely able to muster a smile. He walked past the Armagh panel, who were conducting their warm-down. One of their players muttered, 'It must be the 'Man of the Match' award. The group burst into laughter.

John Joe was gone.

I had no idea what awaited me in the final three or four years of my life as a Donegal footballer. Jim McGuinness was not someone I was giving a moment's thought about.

I'd no idea who would be the next Donegal manager, or the last of the five managers I would spend my time with?

● ● ●

Kathryn had allowed me to take off at the end of 2009. She knew I needed time away. 'I need to get out of here!' I told her, and she knew I had my fill of football. What she did not know was that I would propose to her after she joined me in New York for two weeks over March, as the two of us sat out in the middle of a lake in Central Park; that I had a cheap ring I'd bought off a stall for 10 dollars in my pocket; that I'd almost fall out of the little boat as I tried to go down on one knee and propose to her.

The next day we traipsed down Sixth Avenue and spent the afternoon in jewellers looking for the real thing.

Before then, and in the months that followed, I had managed to get so far away from the Donegal football team. I think John Joe had wanted me to remain as team captain in 2010. He was certainly disappointed when I told him I was about to disappear for a long time.

Myself and Damien started in Bangkok.

Went up through Laos by slow boat on the Mekong River, which was a real eye opener, observing unbelievable poverty and incredible beauty every single day, stopping off in little towns where we spent each night. There was no electricity, no running water, no anything, apart from happy people. Myself and Damien, or Didi as he was always known to me, were filthy dirty by the time we got off the boat for good. We'd also dropped a few pounds, after eating only rice, noodles, or things that occasionally resembled a chicken.

In Luang Prabang, we went tubing on the craziest, most dangerous body of water I could ever have imagined. Didi and I set off, each of us in an inflatable rubber tube, and the Mekong takes you down for miles. Wee bars in huts, built on stilts, dotted the banks. Didi and I only got a few hundred yards down the river.

We grabbed one of the ropes that was thrown into us, and were pulled in. We climbed the homemade ladders, and drank for the day instead. Zip cords swung out into the river. The craic looked brilliant. We had called a halt to our river journey, which was one of our best decisions. We drank our chilled beers, and watched others take their lives in their hands instead.

A wee hospital had been built on the other side of the river. It had to be, because there were so many people who were trying to kill themselves on the zip wires. Health and safety was nonexistent. People were hitting the water at one hundred miles per hour blind drunk.

They were letting go too early.

They were hitting rocks, left and right.

One old boy, while I lay back drinking my beer, was stretched out of the water after smashing his leg on one of the rocks. But there were dozens and dozens of more people queuing up to take the wires back down to the river.

It was the only time on our world tour that I thought of the Donegal football team, and my wish to play for the county again.

In Hanoi, however, I forgot about the team again quickly enough. We hit Hue on motorcycles, and then Da Nang, where the Americans had their biggest air base during the Vietnam war. We travelled the whole way down to Ho Chi Minh city, the old Saigon, and I lapped up every bit of information I could get on the war.

We then did Australia and rented the cheapest and dingiest 'Wicked' camper van we could find in Sydney and drove the whole way up to Cairns and the Great Barrier Reef.

Then New Zealand.

And Fiji. We flew into Los Angeles, made our way to New York. Over the course *of the few months we hadn't taken too many risky moves. But at one stage, people at home in Donegal did hear that I might be in some big trouble.*

As big as it gets, because they were told myself and Didi were caught in the middle of a cyclone. We were on one of the hundreds of islands that make up Fiji. And we were in lockdown in our resort, even though Cyclone Thomas was passing us by, and was a couple of hundred miles away.

At home, however, people thought we were in the middle of the path of this cyclone. The reason they thought that was because we told them.

We had nothing to do with ourselves, apart from lounge by the pool by day and have dinner with a few drinks at night. We got to know the barman very well as you do if you're Irish. He was working in the resort for stints of three and four months at a time before heading back home to his own island, and he loved to phone home.

And each night, Didi and I gave him our phones because we discovered it was not costing us anything. In return we had free drinks all evening long.

The barman had my phone, when a call came through to Didi. 'Are you in the middle of a hurricane over there?' he was asked.

Didi was enjoying his Long Island Iced Teas.

It was another beautifully warm, tranquil evening, with hardly a wisp of air hitting our faces.

The tequila, vodka, rum and gin was working well.

'Aye...' replied Didi.

'We're in the middle of it... right in the centre of it... it's TERRIBLE!'

'Trees are down...

*'Coconuts are flying off the f****** trees!' he continued.*

It was his brother, who works for the BBC, he was talking to.

'Are you serious, Damien?' he was asked.

*'F****** awful...' confirmed Didi.*

Next thing, Didi's brother tells him that Shaun Doherty from Highland Radio wants to have a word with him. His current affairs show has one of the highest listenerships in the county.

So here we were.

Live. On air.

'Didi... don't be doing this!' I warned him.

Doherty's very formal, almost posh accent was the next thing I overheard on Didi's phone as I leaned into the conversation.

There were thousands and thousands of people in Donegal now listening in on our conversation also.

'Damien... Damien... tell me the EXTRAORDINARY story?' asked Doherty, '... what are the conditions like out there?

'How BAD is it, Damien?'

'It's bad,' Didi replied, slurring every second word.

'The thing that we're scared about, is not the wind,' continued Didi, '... or ... erm ... the rain but fallin' ... erm... fallin' coconuts. They're the worst thing that people are afraid of.

'Falling coconuts. Every resort is riddled with coconut trees and a lot of people... they die from coconuts falling every year.'

'How bizarre,' replied Doherty, who was clearly onto us at this stage.

'So, let me get this straight?' said Doherty. 'It's not roofs that are caving in on people's heads that's the danger during this terrible cyclone... it's coconuts falling down and hitting them on the head and killing them?'

'Exactly,' claimed Didi. 'Exactly!'

'I believe,' said Doherty, '... I believe the Donegal footballer, Rory Kavanagh is with you there.

'Can I have a word with Rory?'

I was on the line next.

I actually tried to temper the story, and mentioned to Doherty that Damien and I were in a bunker, about 400 metres underground.

I mentioned that we were tracking the cyclone overhead on our laptop. I tried my best, despite the Iced Teas, and despite Damien's disagreement, to assure Shaun Doherty that we expected to come out of our ordeal alive.

And that was the last we thought of the interview.

● ● ●

Didi took a call by the pool side the next morning from Kathryn. She had been unable to get me on my phone.

I had forgotten to get it back from the barman.

Cyclone Thomas, in retrospect, was the calm. The perfect storm was about to hit.

'WHERE'S RORY?' Kathryn demanded.

'He's okay... he's up in bed!'

'GET HIM... NOW!'

Kathryn was not worried one bit about my safety.

She knew the story.

Damien and I were in the Daily Star newspaper, she informed me. We were headline news.

People were sick to death with worry.

My mother had her Blessed Candles lit all over the house.

Kathryn was not amused.

I was called in after 47 minutes of the Ulster final.

I came in for Christy, and picked Darren Hughes. From there to the end, I was not really part of the game. It was just all about myself and Hughes, as far as I was concerned.

I was doing a man marking job on him, and I was enjoying it. I was burying my shoulder into him every chance I got. Twice, the referee David Coldrick gave me a warning.

I didn't stop.

'I'm watching you!' the ref had told me.

Don't care, I thought to myself.

Watch away!

I was doing more talking than I had done in years. I wanted to annoy him, and hurt him given half the chance. At the same time, I knew that I was not getting into the game myself. I hardly cared.

I had endured the longest and most frustrating year of my life, and Hughes had been party to that, and for the remaining minutes of the Ulster final my single priority was to make him suffer in every possible way.

From the very first minute of the game, I could see that the pendulum had swung back in our direction. We were at full force, unlike the 2013 Ulster final. They were reacting.

We were the aggressors.

They were still reacting, and usually too late.

From that very first minute, any time they got their hands on the ball, our boys were all back into their defensive positions. We were playing the game completely on our terms.

We were telling them to come to us!

Early on, I watched from the sideline as Darren Hughes got on the ball, and started soloing. He kept soloing, and had nowhere to go. He knew he was not going to be able to get a long ball into his full forward line.

Neither were we giving away any free kicks.

Inside our 45 metres line, there was nothing being given for free, for Conor McManus or Kieran Hughes. Not as much as an inch of room for free. We had our fill of Monaghan, and we had prepared for them.

They knew they had no option but to run the ball.

And they were going to have to run the ball into a wall. At breakdowns, our boys were seizing every moment and breaking at speed. It was inspiring to watch. We were back to normal. We were energised.

I waited for the first half to end.

I knew we were going to win.

Monaghan did not have the quality of running game that we possessed. We had refined our running game since 2011. They, in comparison, were still on a learning curve. From the beginning that was obvious, from the first few minutes, and I ached to be part of it, but at the same time I was excited and amazed at the brilliance of all of our boys.

As we left the Slieve Russell Hotel, McGuinness had mentioned to me that I should be ready to come in.

That was no consolation to me. I had almost felt embarrassed all through the morning. Sitting down to eat with the rest of the team, I felt that I had eyes on me. When the team was announced a few hours before the game, I did not want to look anyone in the face. I did not want to talk with anybody.

I wanted my own space on the bus.

I was angry with myself, and angry with McGuinness, and I guess by the time I got onto the field midway through the second half I was in some sort of crazed state of mind.

The McGees were in full warrior mode at the back for us.

Big Neil was in command in the middle

Up front we won our free kicks, where we wanted to win them, and Murph and Colm kicked six of them during the afternoon. When Paddy McBrearty came in after 26 minutes, he found more freedom than the other two boys, and kicked three big points.

The game began and ended entirely to our plan, on our terms. We led from start to finish. It was 0-15 to 1-9 at the final whistle.

We were back exactly where we wanted to be. Back out on the empty pitch in Clones with the Anglo Celt Cup sitting in front of us we stood for our team photo.

Redemption was ours.

The team coach pulled in by the side of the road, and Jim McGuinness crossed the road with the Anglo Celt Cup in his hand.

We all watched, as we always did, silently. McGuinness gently placed the cup in front of the wooden cross on the other side of the road, that made sacred the place where his brother Mark had died as he drove Jim to the airport for a summer of football in the United States so many years before.

Like he had done after the Ulster final victories in 2011 and 2012, and after the All-Ireland win, McGuinness stood there motionless.

CHAPTER  13

I knew I was going to get game time against Armagh.

Once again, my name was missing when McGuinness called out the team the morning of our All-Ireland quarter final. As always, he liked to keep everything under lock and key until the last hour before we left our hotel in Johnstown House. At that same time, mobile phones were also offered up by all of us.

McGuinness did not want any distractions. Neither did he want anyone foolishly leaking any information, to anybody. But, this time, I had been tuned to the vibes in training the days beforehand and the naming of the team was less of a kick in the gut for me.

As the boys were leaving the hotel, I ducked into the toilet.

When I came out, I found myself walking towards the team bus with McGuinness. That's when he told me I would be going in against Armagh.

But, that was when he also told me something else.

'You are going to be starting against Dublin!'

I was a little shocked.

We had a quarter final still to win, before Dublin came into view in the semi final. We had a lot to do first of all.

'You will be playing from the start against Dublin,' he continued, as we reached the door of the bus.

'That's the game I need you ready for!'

He told me that Big Neil would be playing somewhere else at the start of the game against Dublin.

'... you are going well again in training... I can see it in your legs!'

He gave me a pat on the back.

And walked on.

The quarter final did not go to plan.

We found ourselves in a game we had never fully imagined. Armagh had always torn up our best laid plans, as far back as I could remember. They'd only lost to us once in 10 games going back to 1999. They liked playing us, and McGeeney knew in his heart that Armagh could always beat us.

In the last round of the Qualifiers they had 10 different scorers in their five points win over Meath. They kicked 18 points on a rotten night for football. Stefan Campbell, Aidan Forker, and Tony Kernan did most of the damage for them around the middle winning and turning over ball.

We were prepared for a bit of a war in Croke Park on the Saturday afternoon, and we knew we might need to be patient. They were not going to roll over. But nothing prepared us for being one point down with two minutes left on the clock. I had come into the game after 43 minutes for Christy.

Every ball was being fought for with a serious intensity from the first minute. There were skirmishes. One big shoving match on the field included our 'flying doc'.

However, although we did not play our very best and totalled 15 wides, which was inexcusable and showed that our shot selection was way off, we remained calm. Armagh ran into a whole different Donegal team than the team that always panicked and got all hot and bothered over the previous 15 years. We kept working the ball.

Keeping it.

Stretching them, doing everything we knew off by heart in training. We knew there was no need to do anything different. There was no point.

I felt I had made a good impact when I came in. I ran at them a couple of times and drew frees. By the end, I felt that I had helped to change the momentum of the game. And afterwards, the boys were complimentary. Neil McGee was one of the first to come over to me.

'Well done... we needed you out there!'

It was good to hear. They all knew that I was down and that I had gone through a tough time, and that my confidence was rocked. Their words were a shot in the arm for me.

I needed all of the encouragement I could get.

At half time, McGuinness had a lot of work to do, and more to say. He gave out to Christy for not doing the man marking job on Aaron Kernan he had been ordered to do. When I went in for Christy, I was told to give us our full defensive shape. They were getting too much joy up our flanks. McGuinness felt that Christy had been too high up the field on his man.

Eamon McGee also got an earful.

He was supposed to me taking up Campbell. But, instead, he found himself on Kevin Dyas, and had picked him up instead. That decision of Eamon's had done McGuinness' head in.

'You were assigned to him!

'Why did you not take him... what's wrong with you?' demanded McGuinness. Eamon fought his corner.

'He came into me... I couldn't leave Dyas inside, could I?' he replied to McGuinness.

'If I went out on Campbell what was going to happen?'

McGuinness put his foot down.

Campbell scored a fortunate enough goal for them in the 60th minute. The ball hit the woodwork, and then went in off the leg of Papa.

That could have been curtains for us.

But Murph hit a magnificent point with his left foot, and then Paddy struck one that was equally sweet with his right foot.

We were one point up. The game was just about up, though they had two late opportunities, two frees from Tony Kernan which were just about outside his range. Both fell short.

The semi final, as much as anything else, was going to be a battle between

Papa and Stephen Cluxton.

McGuinness warned us in the weeks leading into the game against Dublin that he had examined every single kick out Cluxton had taken all year long, and he could not identify any patterns.

He admitted that Cluxton was that good. Cluxton was seeing to it that Dublin got up to 80% retention of the ball from every kick, explained McGuinness. It was an incredible return.

But Papa too was remarkable in finding men from the placed ball. He had worked so hard to become one of the best goalkeepers in the game, and he was as good as Cluxton with kick outs, perhaps better?

From the beginning of 2014, McGuinness spent a lot of time working on our kick outs. He had our goalkeepers hitting hundreds and hundreds of balls every week into different zones of the field.

Repetition.

Repetition... repetition.

Before training. After training.

Ultimately, Papa could hit the ball anywhere. He could land it on a sixpence out the field if McGuinness wanted him to do so. His range of kicks was unbelievable. He could do daisy-cutters.

He could cut one out to the left, when he was actually positioned to kick it to the right and was looking in that direction.

For a man his size, Papa had a serious pair of brilliant feet.

For his club, Four Masters, the same club as Karlo who served as Best Man at his wedding, Papa often lined out in the middle of the field, and up at full forward.

It was hard for anybody to get a ball by him. In a one on one situation, even in training, he was able to fill his goals. There was no massive agility about him, like some of the boys who play in goals in England, but Gaelic football is so different to soccer. In that game they are making saves down around their ankles most of the time.

Gaelic football is different.

Shay Given found that out fairly quickly when he joined us in training that summer in Convoy. The balls were whistling past his head into the net.

'Jesus boys... I'm used to them down here!' he told us, pointing to the ground, to

the left and right of him.

Shay was a good bloke with us and so supportive, and it was amazing to have such a successful footballer with us. But, at times I felt a little sorry for him. We were playing four on four, so there were a lot of shots going at him.

The balls were being banged left, right and centre, and most of them were going in, some of them whistling into the top corners. After two minutes of the first game, we went to change teams.

Shay was standing there.

His hands on his hips, shaking his head and laughing.

Papa, in contrast, was well able to save balls that were anything above waist high. He just batted them down most of the time.

Papa had the safest pair of hands, and the most trustworthy feet of any man on the Donegal team.

That's why, what happened to him in the All-Ireland final, when he inexplicably chipped his kick out into the hands of an unmarked Kieran Donaghy standing right in front of him, was such a freak event.

McGuinness likened Dublin to Chelsea Football Club, in the Roman Abramovich era. He was happy to tell reporters that the divide between the very top teams and the others was widening, and that Dublin were leading that charge faster and bolder than anyone else.

He cited the county's size. Their money. The jobs they had for their boys. The coaching systems and support network.

'The level that they have taken sports science to...' stated McGuinness. 'Nutrition, conditioning, the amount of coaches they have... it's a professional set up in every aspect.'

Meanwhile, in Donegal, a decision had been made to build a Centre of Excellence in Convoy. A new football home for the county that would have it all.

Money, however, was a problem.

Donegal did not have the funds available, not like Tyrone for instance.

And the Centre of Excellence was not fully completed.

At one County Board meeting, the future of the site which was to become the fully completed Centre of Excellence was being discussed. At the back of the room, was a little lad who had been brought to the meeting by his father, one of the County Board officers.

The young lad was obviously listening in to what was being said because I'm told at one point, after a break in the debate, he piped up from the back of the room. All heads turned to hear what he had to say for himself.

'Centre of Excellence...?' he said

'More like ... a...

'...CENTRE OF MIDDLING'

On the Tuesday evening after beating Armagh, McGuinness had us training in Convoy. Half of us took up one portacabin serving as a dressing room. The other half were in a second portacabin.

'Centre of Middling....!'

We all liked to remind one another of the verdict of the little lad at the meeting. The whole county got to know about the Centre of Middling.

Jim called us all into one of the portacabins.

It was a bit of a squeeze.

'Centre of Middling...!' someone whispered.

And everyone laughed once again.

When everyone was finally inside, it was a complete squash, but McGuinness was perfectly happy. He wanted to talk to us about Dublin.

'I know how to beat Dublin,' he began.

And he continued for the next 20 minutes explaining to us, and convincing us, that he had worked out exactly how it was going to be done.

'I've been tracking them all year!' he told us, more than once in that 20 minutes.

'It's all bullshit...

'All this talk of them being the team nobody can beat.

'... it's BULLSHIT!'

When he was finished, he left the room and told us to talk about Dublin amongst ourselves for another 10 minutes.

By then, he had poured out his belief that we would beat them. 'We are going to be ready for these boys,' he stressed. '... mark my words!'

Before he left, McGuinness had even admitted to us that he was getting the look from members of his own family that Donegal were going to be in big trouble in the semi final.

'I am getting the impression from my own family... that they are nervous. And if I am feeling that... from my own family, then every one of you are feeling it as well from your own families.

'It's bullshit.

'It's all hype.

'They haven't faced anything like they are going to face against us!'

In the 24 hours after we had beaten Armagh, everyone I had spoken with could not help themselves from bringing up Dublin. And it was so true, they all sounded concerned.

As we spoke amongst ourselves, we promised that we were going to have the best training session we had ever had that same evening. We all said we were going to give it everything out on the pitch, from that very first evening.

And we did have our greatest training session.

We launched into every single drill at 200 miles per hour. The intensity was amazing. Nobody held back. I was hyped up more than anyone. I was back on the team. The other boys did not know that.

But I did.

We told ourselves it was going to be the greatest game of our lives.

The single greatest moment.

We were cast as sad underdogs.

Dublin were presented as the team that was saving the soul of Gaelic football, with their positive, daring, breathtaking attacking play.

They were seen as the good guys!

We were seen as something evil, even still.

We loved that match up.

Good V's Evil?

Except we were convinced that we were going to beat the team that was rampaging through every other team, and tearing every opponent apart limb from limb.

On the morning of the game, McGuinness turned Mystic Meg.

Once again.

On the flipchart beside him he had written down numbers.

Two or three goals.

16 or 17 points.

That's what he had written down.

And he pointed to the numbers.

'This score is achievable today!' he announced.

It was the same message he had been giving us in training every week.

McGuinness's tactical breakdown of what would happen against Dublin was almost perfect in 2011.

Back then, it was about keeping the numbers down. This time, though, the emphasis had shifted. It was how he had planned our evolution – our four-year cycle. 'The Olympic Cycle' as he would later term it.

We weren't being told what to do to stop Dublin – now we would see if they could stop us.

'There are goals in this game!' he promised.

'They are going to press high... once we get beyond the surge, we are into open country... have you got that?

'I am watching them on videos all of the time... every game... the bad teams are getting nose bleeds when they get free and get into room...

'Those other teams find themselves in space... in the middle of Croke Park, the noise, the pressure, they think they have to kick the ball...

'... and they kick it down the throat of O'Carroll and Cooper!'

He was telling us this, and he was working on what he was telling us in training.

He set up a particular drill. The man was told to solo alone down the field towards the full forward line, where Murph or Colm was marked one-on-one by a defender. The man in possession had to make the best use he could of possession, with the inside forward trying to get free of the defender, who was marking out in front. If the pass wasn't on, the ball-carrier was encouraged to go on and pop over his score.

In turn, every single evening, all of us found ourselves on dozens of runs down the middle of the field, nobody near us, running headlong towards our full forward line.

Soloing... and looking up.

Seeing Murph and Colm and Paddy, and seeing defenders two or three yards in front of each forward. McGuinness wanted us to develop our decision making on the ball. As we raced down the field, he told us we were in Croke Park.

'You've broken through Dublin's high surge... and you're on the ball... you're on your own...!' he told us.

'What are you going to do with the ball?'

In the first couple of sessions, all of us, every last man, was absolutely brutal in making the right decision. Again and again, a man was running through, nobody near him, and he was soloing the ball, looking up, soloing again, and every time he kicked it when he did not need to kick it.

'This is what bad teams do...' McGuinness announced. 'This is what bad teams have been doing against Dublin in Croke Park... and here we are in training, and we're doing the same thing!'

Eamon McGee and Paddy McGrath were winning the ball in front.

Every single evening, McGuinness had us making those runs.

Repetition.

Repetition... repetition.

He wanted us to do the right thing on the ball.

He wanted us to visualise running down the middle of Croke Park. Nobody near the man on the ball.

Either delay the pass?

Wait for the forward to come?

Wait for the forward to make one run, two runs?

Wait for him to make three runs?

Wait, and have the patience, have the composure, to wait longer? Wait until the pass is definitely on?

All of this became ingrained in us.

Then the next phase of the movement.

What if the pass is not on?

What then?

Keep running.

Wait and keep running?

Run and keep running until the ball is run to completion?

'There are goals in this game...' McGuinness assured us, over and over. 'There's goals in this game, and we are going to get goals from our kick outs.

'We are going to suck them in.'

We would beat Dublin playing the way we had been training for those weeks. And we would score three goals and 14 points in our semi final win.

Jimmy Tunes?

Mustic Meg?

Jim McGuinness.

When we ran out onto Croke Park, finally, Neil McGee sprinted down to the Hill 16 end of the ground where the Dublin support was biggest and noisiest, as always. He was pumped up. I had never seen him so pumped up.

He was barging his way out of the dressing room, almost pushing boys out of the way. He almost crashed by Murph at the door.

Then, once out there, he tore towards the Hill.

He stood there, arms by his side and fists clenched just staring at the Hill. He had a little smile on his face as if to say... *I'm ready.. show me your worst!*

It was like he was asking the Dublin supporters on the Hill something.

Where's this Brogan fella... where is he?

That's what he seemed to be saying.

McGuinness had built a U stretching out from our goalmouth. It stretched 40 metres either side of Papa's goal, and reached out to the 45 metres line.

This is ours, he had declared.

'Dublin do not score inside this U.'

CHAPTER

Dublin's game was based on volume.

According to McGuinness, with Cluxton's retention rate from his kick outs so high, by far the highest in the country, and with Dublin owning so much ball, and doing so much hard running with the ball, everyone chasing in support, their opponents simply feel overwhelmed.

'Teams can not deal with it!' determined McGuinness

'It wears them down...!

'Guard this U... guard it with your lives...

'... and they'll not be able to score!

'And even if they flash over a few from long range... that's not sustainable.'

End of story, according to Jim McGuinness.

Nobody gave us a chance in hell.

From the throw-in, I received the ball and made a dart at goal and, for a split second, I thought a goal was on. As I turned I was cleaned from behind by a high challenge from James McCarthy. He went in the book and Murph tapped over the first score of the game.

But Dublin asserted themselves and took control for 25 minutes.

They led 0-9 to 0-4. Maybe we were 7/1 with bookmakers for a reason?

At one stage I was put out over the line at the Davin End and almost ended up on my arse. There was a cheer from the Dublin supporters behind the goals.

Jesus, I thought. *This could be one long day.*

I kicked a bad wide soon after but thankfully, from the very next play, I managed to grasp a ball at the second attempt and steer it over the Dublin crossbar.

We were defending our U.

Dublin did not seem to give a damn, and they spent the first 25 minutes kicking points from everywhere and anywhere outside the U.

Paul Flynn kicked three of them.

Diarmuid Connolly banged over three mighty shots of his own.

Cluxton was running the whole game with the excellence of his kick outs, and in the 23rd minute he had flighted the ball magnificently onto the path of Alan Brogan and he had planted another unbelievable point over the bar. We were being destroyed.

Our U was also not quite working.

They had goal chances too.

In the 12th minute Eoghan O'Gara raced in on goal and flicked a pass to Bernard Brogan who should have scored, only the pass was behind him.

They had a second goal chance when Connolly was set up by Cormac Costello, but Papa made a fantastic save.

The game could have been over by half time.

They had banged over big score, after big score, the sort that can knock the stuffing out of most teams. Even if one of those goal chances had gone in, we might not have been able to pick ourselves up off the ground.

The doubts were settling into our heads. We were protecting McGuinness' U, but each of us wanted to push out, and get up the field and stop them from getting their free shots at goal. At the same time, we knew that if we did push up, Brogan and O'Gara inside would have enough room to potentially cut our throat.

I was not sure what was going to happen next?

Christy, for starters, was thrown in by Jim. He started putting in his big tackles as usual, and be made a couple of his strong runs down the field. Christy Toye was always a tonic for us. He made one big tackle on Michael Darragh Macauley, won the ball from him and raced down the other end.

The ovation from the crowd stunned us all.

In the next 10 minutes, everything changed. By half time we were in front by a single point, 1-8 to 0-10. By the time Flynn shot over Dublin's 10th point just before the break, we were not just a different team, we were the team that had spent all those weeks working on breaking Dublin down.

Now we were doing just that.

We scored 1-4 without reply. We had claimed the first of the many goals McGuinness had promised us we would find. It was not exactly like one of the goals we had worked on religiously on the training ground. Those goals would come in the second half. Exactly as McGuinness had told us.

The first goal came when I picked up possession just under the Hogan Stand. I jinked inside and hit a long ball into the square, hoping to find Murph.

Murph made a nuisance of himself and managed to put in a tackle on a Cluxton. He fumbled the ball and Colm picked up the pieces. He off loaded the ball to Ryan McHugh, who had gambled in racing forward, and found the ball breaking perfectly for him. He stuck it in the net.

In those 10 minutes, our heads were calmed.

Meanwhile, Dublin's were left spinning. Towards the end of the half, Flynn and Connolly missed efforts that beforehand had sailed over. Maybe those long range efforts were unsustainable after all?

Our second goal came four minutes into the second half.

It was Ryan McHugh again who finished it off, after Anthony Thompson had initially supported Eamon McGee down the right wing and then calmly carried the ball deep into the Dublin defence, drawing three of their men to him as he did so. Tony found himself in space and with half a chance. He was held up by Cian O'Sullivan but held his head, turned inside, and set up Ryan who palmed the ball home.

Our third goal came in the 47th minute.

Myself and Murph competed for a long kick out from Papa. Murph flicked the ball down in the middle.

Big Neil gathered it and gave it to Odhran who carried it forward, and it ended with Colm McFadden side-stepping Cluxton and banging it home.

It was game over.

Dublin's game plan collapsed on them.

All through the second half they were playing like a broken team. Their confidence was down around their ankles. Up front, they began to panic, and the more they fretted and second-guessed themselves on the ball, the more the panic dug deep.

They were a team with no Plan B.

For some of Papa's kick outs, only Cluxton and Colm McFadden and Mick Fitzsimons were actually stationed in the Dublin half of the field. Everybody else in blue was pushed right up the field.

And Papa started booming those kicks.

Any time we won a ball in the second half around the middle and looked up the field, we could see the same long empty road, though it was more of a highway actually, in front of us that McGuinness had promised us in training we would find.

All we had to do was carry the ball

And avoid any nose bleeds.

In losing to us, in their 11th championship game under Jim Gavin, Dublin had recorded their lowest score ever.

Our tally of 3-14 was also the highest score they had conceded in those same number of games. In no game had Dublin ever gone 10 minutes without getting some score.

However, in losing on this occasion, they had two 10 minute periods, one in each half, when they got nothing out of the game, not even a sniff at a point. Never before in those 11 games had Dublin failed to score a goal.

The breakdown of the head to head between Papa and Cluxton also told the story of the game perfectly. Papa had beaten him in kick outs retained, 16-15. And in goals conceded Papa had a 3-0 victory.

McGuinness also had his greatest day as one of the game's true geniuses. If we had just watched a game of tennis, then Jim had out-gunned Jim Gavin 6-4, 6-0, 6-0, or something along those lines.

From the very start, Jim had decided to make the semi final a game that was played on Donegal's terms, and he insisted on having Big Neil and Murph in the middle for the throw up. He wanted to lay down a warning that his team were intent on winning every single battle, beginning with the first ball thrown into the air.

I started the game inside on the full forward line, but almost immediately I was out there and taking up Macauley.

Big Neil moved in the opposite direction and grabbed all of their attention as he positioned himself in front of Cluxton's goal. McGuinness wanted to mess with their heads, on the field and on the sideline.

Even though Cluxton favours his half backs, and Flynn, Connolly and O'Sullivan in particular with his kick outs, and Macauley was not one of the natural targets, I was still on a mission to beat their biggest and strongest man in the middle of the field. McGuinness knew as well as I did, that Macauley never wanted to be touched. Especially off kick outs I was giving him some close attention.

As expected, Macauley became agitated.

He became all elbows and forearms. His late uncle Leo was from Lettermacaward in Donegal and had delivered me into this world. I doubt whether Michael Darragh knew that.

We were going at it a bit. Nothing over the top, just a bit of pulling and dragging.

Cluxton, however, was so fast with some of his kick outs. Early on, there were occasions when I was arriving back where I was supposed to be and a Dublin forward already was taking his shot at goal.

The long kick out did an incredible amount of damage against Dublin. They had so many men pushing high up the field, man on man, that Papa's bombs took them all out of the play.

It was a 'win win' kick out for us.

With Papa's kicks sailing over their heads, the Dublin defenders were seriously confused. The worry on their faces was easy to pick up as well.

They had been programmed to go 'man to man', and they knew there was nothing behind them, just a wide open space and all the room in the world for us to run into if we won the ball.

They had nobody at home.

Good Guys V's Bad Guys?

The Good Guys were made to look foolish, and naive, and the Bad Guys? The Donegal football team was suddenly the toast of the country after defying odds which were decreed insurmountable.

We'd also scored three goals and 14 points in the most daring, courageous, brilliantly rehearsed performance ever seen in the modern game most probably. We were no longer so bad!

However, we were suddenly hot favourites to win the All-Ireland title again. We were going for our third All-Ireland. Kerry were going for their 37th, but they were allowed to take up the role of underdogs.

Kerry had also found out so many positives about themselves in their two semi final games against Mayo. They looked like a beaten team in the drawn semi final, but Kieran Donaghy was sent in and he saved his team's neck.

Donaghy was suddenly his old self again, and with James O'Donoghue looking as dangerous as Colm Cooper, and also looking perfectly happy with his role as his team's deadly assassin up front in Cooper's absence, Kerry came into the final twice as strong as they had come into the semi final.

In their semi final replay win over Mayo in Limerick their manager, Eamon Fitzmaurice had used a total of 23 players during the course of the game itself and extra time. It was a young Kerry team, and nine of their boys would be playing in an All-Ireland final for the first time, but they were a team coming right into their best form just as the season was about to end.

And, still, we were raging hot favourites.

Even though, with their two big games with Mayo behind them, Kerry had a scoring average of 1-19 per game in 2014. Our average was 1-16.

But, McGuinness did not mind the pressure that was coming down on our shoulders. He always believed in never worrying about finals.

'The final will take care of itself, boys!'

It was a promise he would repeat to us more than once as we prepared for the All-Ireland final.

We did our training camp in the Lough Erne Resort in Fermanagh. There was a lot of DVD work. We trained in the mornings, and then came back to the hotel for our recovery. Ice baths and some relaxation time in the pool. Everyone napped. Then back to the field for a late afternoon session. Adam Speer and Eugene Eivers, our strength and conditioning coaches, took us for some light stretching and made sure we were fully recovered from one session to the next.

And more DVDs. We watched Kerry round the clock.

We watched the Munster final where they had hammered Cork 0-24 to 0-12 in Páirc Uí Chaoimh, and both of their games against Mayo. With McGuinness holding the remote control, and stopping games every 60 seconds to talk through a play, a 70 minute game usually stretched itself out to something like 150 minutes.

As a group, we had talked and talked about Kerry, their defensive line in front of their 45, and Murph and Colm dragging Aidan O'Mahony and Marc O Se out so we could dink a ball in behind to our runners coming from deep.

David Moran had been heroic for them in the middle against Mayo, and he needed watching. Johnny Buckley was a serious workhorse for them in the middle as well, but my job was to take up Anthony Maher.

The weeks flew by, unlike 2012.

Then the days flew by.

Eamon McGee was living and working in Letterkenny for over a year, and he would normally call up to my house two or three times a week. Usually twice during weekdays for training, and then again at weekends, the day before we left for a game.

The day before the All-Ireland final, on the Saturday morning, he had called to collect me before we headed to the Mount Errigal Hotel to jump on the team bus that was taking us down to Johnstown House Hotel in County

Meath. But when he arrived at the house I was a total mess.

I had woken up to discover my throat was closed over. I had trouble swallowing and there were white spots on the back of my throat!

What the hell is this? I thought.

And... why now!

I was in a state of panic. I was searching the medicine cabinet for tablets but I couldn't find the right ones. I rang the Doc, Charlie McManus. I must of sounded like a mad man.

'Jesus Charlie, my throat has completely closed over!' I told him.

'I can barely swallow and... there are these white spots on the back of my throat!'

'Don't worry...' Charlie replied.

'... you're grand ... you'll be fine!'

Charlie had the ability to put anyone at ease straight away. He had that especially protective way with him.

'I'll get a look at ya in Donegal Town...' he continued. 'But I'm telling you it won't keep you out. I' ll give you something for it...

'... and you'll be fine for tomorrow!

'Okay?'

Kathryn in the meantime had been on the phone to our mate, Arlene Devenney and told her of my plight. Women can get things done quickly, and I mean quickly. Because no sooner had Kathryn hung up the phone, than Arlene was at our front door holding a jug that was covered in tinfoil.

'What's that?' I asked.

'It's a special brew for sore throats... get it into ya on the way down the road,' she ordered.

When I took the jug out and unfolded the tin foil wrapping on the bus in Letterkenny the boys were thinking I had gone funny in the head. It looked like a green sludge in the jug.

And the smell was horrific. It was rough.

'What the hell is that?' one or two of them asked.

'Don't ask'!

I started downing this dreadful mixture.

I never found out what it was either.

By the time I reached Donegal Town for lunch my throat felt a hundred times better. Together with the medication from our Doc, I actually started to eat my lunch.

I could swallow my food.

By the time I reached Johnstown House Hotel, I was perfectly fine again. The drama had all but disappeared.

We were rocked in the opening minute of the game. We would be rocked, again, in the 52nd minute.

After all of our planning, so little went to plan in the All-Ireland final. All of the hard work we had done on the training field, and yet we were unable to summon up all of our reserves of energy to give the ultimate performance against Kerry. We found out that All-Ireland finals can be strange beasts.

The final did not take care of itself.

Neil McGee would hold James O'Donoghue scoreless over the 70 minutes, and if we had been told that the evening before, then we would have been even more certain of winning back the Sam Maguire Cup. O'Donoghue spent more time out the field than he spent in their inside forward line, sniffing and poaching about our goalmouth.

It was a brave tactical plan by Eamon Fitzmaurice.

However, even though O'Donoghue got nothing, Kerry totalled two goals and three points, all from play, from their full forward line. The first of those two goals came inside 60 seconds. Paul Geaney was isolated on Paddy McGrath. Stephen O'Brien's attempted shot was partially blocked by Karlo and the ball dropped short at the edge of the square. Geaney caught it clean over Paddy's head.

And Geaney squeezed his shot into the net at the Davin End. Kieran Donaghy kicked a point after four minutes, but they would only score two more points before half time. That's how well we defended.

That much worked for us. I tried bringing the fight to them on a couple of occasions. Once I managed to play a ball through to Darach O'Connor, who was a surprise inclusion, but unfortunately Jigger's shot went agonisingly beyond the far post and wide. It was only a matter of inches after the merest of deflections off the goalkeeper.

Kerry also had numbers back, and we needed three expertly kicked frees from Murph to stay close with them during the first quarter. It was 1-3 to 0-6 at half time.

We were not ourselves, but we still had an All-Ireland title at our fingertips. We had been flat and lethargic in the first half. We expected the second half to be an entirely different story.

The second half was even more confusing and frustrating than the first, however. We took the lead in the 38th minute. They inched back in front, and when Donaghy scored their second goal, we fought back with a vengeance immediately. We scored three points in three minutes.

But we were still not playing well.

They were getting too much possession in the middle. They dominated that middle third, and that is where we would ultimately lose the All-Ireland final. We didn't do enough damage on their kick outs and we were losing the battle for breaking ball... simple as that.

There was one point in it.

It still felt like a game we would win. Even though we were still spilling the ball and presenting too many turnovers, we had taken two giant blows to the chin, and we were still standing. We just needed a foothold in the game.

Their wing back Paul Murphy went forward and struck a fine point. Then Johnny Buckley added a point that was just as good. We were three points down, and the game was almost out of our grasp.

Deep into injury time, Murph bore down on the Kerry goal. He was unstoppable as he raced through. Murph flicked the ball to Paddy McBrearty, who had scored two points when he came in for Ryan McHugh in the middle of the half. Paddy's shot was deflected. Colm McFadden threw himself at the ball.

Colm got his hand to the ball.

It clipped off the bottom of the post.

That was our last chance.

In the 52nd minute Kerry had been handed their second goal.

Papa had handed it to them personally. It was tragic for him, and it was a blood-curdling body-blow for the rest of us.

I was jogging out towards the middle of the field. I was pulling wide, and thinking of the kick out from Papa, and I had just turned around.

At that moment, everything froze.

Papa went to make a short kick.

Donaghy was in the middle of the D in front of our large square, totally illegally, waving his arms. And Papa kicked the ball to him.

Everything stopped when Donaghy got the ball.

There was nobody near him. The defence had spread, and as usual we were already looking to launch our next attack.

We had worked a lot on short kick outs.

In one, we pushed a fourth man back into the full back line, and got the four men to spread wide, stretching out to the touchline on either side, so that Kerry would not be able to pick up each of the four. Karlo was the fourth man who had dropped back.

We had worked that kick out tirelessly in training.

Papa skewed his kick.

I looked at Donaghy with the ball.

It seemed to take him an age to do anything with it.

It was an eerie moment when the ball hit the back of the net. I could hear no sound in the stadium. It was like I was enveloped in complete silence. And then, only then, was there an explosion of noise in the stadium.

Donaghy, who was not even getting his game for Kerry all summer long! He'd saved Kerry's skin when thrown in against Mayo in the semi final as Fitzmaurice gambled.

Donaghy's career had looked over until then.

But he had just scored the winning goal in the 2014 All-Ireland final. He had scored 1-2, and Kerry were All-Ireland champions, 2-9 to 0-12.

In the players' lounge under the Hogan Stand afterwards, I spoke with Marc O Se. We had studied together in Maynooth.

Kathryn and I had gone down to Ventry and stayed in the family home after the 2002 All-Ireland final. His uncle Páidí won eight All-Irelands and ran a famous bar but that week in Kerry, there was no celebration. They'd lost to Armagh.

It was like a wake.

That's what lay ahead for us now in 2014.

'I know how you feel,' Marc said. 'I've lost four All-Ireland finals.'

In the back of my mind, I wasn't going to lose another one as I was ready to retire. I had been ready for 12 months, and the inexplicable, sickening defeat in the All-Ireland final was not something that was going to change my mind. Even though I had absolutely no idea, not until the minute we had lost, how gut wrenching a defeat in the very last game of the season would prove to be.

The evening of the defeat in the Citywest Hotel outside Dublin was long, and every single minute more insufferable in its complete emptiness than the last.

There were 3,000 people there. The morning after the defeat was far worse. But, I had decided to live with my decision.

I would live with my last game.

So many people I met the evening of the defeat, and the days that followed, wanted to talk about our semi final against Dublin. Our heroic performance. The greatest single performance we had ever given. I did not wish to hear anything about it.

Nobody did.

The long evening after the All-Ireland final, the bus journey home the next day, sitting in pubs, sing-songs, tears, and hugs.

The days that followed were the longest days of my life. I was with my team mates. We needed to be together. We did not need anyone else.

We felt we had let people down.

We were in the depths of misery, but together, in that awful place, it was still good to be with this same group of footballers. All we wanted was one another's company.

Since the beginning of 2014, the whole year long, we had talked amongst ourselves of making one last great stand. We all spoke openly about one last great effort. It was accepted, amongst us, that by the end of 2014 we would no longer exist as one team.

In team huddles, we spoke about one more year.

Before each championship game, and especially as we prepared for Dublin, and when we had beaten Dublin, we talked about making it the perfect year that would cap all of our careers.

But, I never said my goodbye to the other boys.

I never shook one hand.

I never said good luck to those staying on.

And, I never spoke to Jim McGuinness. We were in one another's company, for the longest three days of our lives, and I never once put my hand out to him.

Or thanked him deeply, and personally.

And I have never met the man since.

Jim McGuinness?

Jimmy Tunes?

Even in defeat some 6,000 people gathered in the Diamond in Donegal Town, as the heavy rain crackled off the umbrellas once again.

Most of us were welling up.

There was always a bond between the team and our supporters, but that murky night in Donegal Town it was stronger than ever.

Jim McGuinness, from day one, set out to restore pride in Donegal football.

Build a team that the people would follow and be proud to follow.

McGuinness took the microphone.

'It's been just phenomenal to work with them and I just want everyone in Donegal tonight to acknowledge them… and hopefully there's a lot more to come from them as well,' he said with a solemn stare.

McGuinness was always about the group.

We won together and we lost together. He had formed that group and there we were, shoulder to shoulder with our people.

Just then, it dawned on me that Jim McGuinness had fully accomplished what he had set out to do.

Pride had been restored.

I was honoured to be part of that.

Massively proud.

My mind wandered back to our first team meeting in Downings in 2010...

'This is Donegal...
'These are our people!
'Out there...
'This is who we are!'

WITHDRAWN STOCK WEXFORD PUBLIC LIBRARIES

BUNCLODY

ENNISCORTHY

GOREY

MOBILE NORTH

MOBILE SOUTH

NEW ROSS

WEXFORD 0 5 JAN 20